Music Theory

FOR DUMMIES

A Wiley Brand

3rd Edition

by Michael Pilhofer, MM and Holly Day

Music Theory For Dummies®, 3rd Edition

Published by: **John Wiley & Sons, Inc.,** 111 River Street, Hoboken, NJ 07030-5774, www.wiley.com

Copyright © 2015 by John Wiley & Sons, Inc., Hoboken, New Jersey

Published simultaneously in Canada

For general information on our other products and services, please contact our Customer Care Department within the U.S. at 877-762-2974, outside the U.S. at 317-572-3993, or fax 317-572-4002. For technical support, please visit www.wiley.com/techsupport.

Wiley publishes in a variety of print and electronic formats and by print-on-demand. Some material included with standard print versions of this book may not be included in e-books or in print-on-demand. If this book refers to media such as a CD or DVD that is not included in the version you purchased, you may download this material at http://booksupport.wiley.com. For more information about Wiley products, visit www.wiley.com.

Library of Congress Control Number: 2014954679

ISBN 978-1-118-99094-0 (pbk); ISBN 978-1-118-899113-8 (ebk); ISBN 978-1-118-899114-5

10 9 8 7 6 5 4 3 2 1

Contents at a Glance

Table of Contents

Introduction

What do you think of when you hear the phrase *music theory*? Does the image of your elementary school music teacher eyeing you from behind the piano pop into your head? Or perhaps you have flashbacks to a later image of fellow college students in theory classes determinedly trying to notate theremin whistles? If either of these ideas is anything close to your own perception of what music theory is, hopefully this book will be a pleasant surprise.

For many self-taught musicians, the idea of theory seems daunting and even a little self-defeating. After all, if you can already read guitar tabs and play some scales, why would you want to muddle what you already know with theory?

Even the most basic music theory training gives you the information you need to expand your range and abilities as a musician. A decent amount of note-reading ability enables you to play a particular type of music, whereas some basic knowledge about chord progressions can help you write your own music.

About This Book

Music Theory For Dummies, 3rd Edition, is designed to give you everything you need to know to become fluent at knocking out a solid beat, reading musical scores, and learning to anticipate where a song should go, whether you're reading someone else's music or writing your own.

Each chapter is as self-contained as possible. In other words, you don't have to read every single chapter to understand what the next one is talking about. Reading the chapters consecutively does help, though, because knowledge of music builds from simple concepts to complex ones.

We cover a lot of territory in this book, from discovering the basics of note values and time signatures to dissecting lead lines and adding harmony to a melody to studying the standard forms that much of popular and classical music follow. So if you're new to the world of music theory, pace yourself while reading this book. Read it while you're sitting at your piano or with your guitar or whatever instrument you're working with next to you, and stop every couple of pages to practice the information you read. If you were taking a music class, this book would cover several years' worth of information, so if you don't learn everything in one or two months, you should refrain from self-flagellation.

Foolish Assumptions

We assume that if you're reading this book, you love music, you want desperately to understand music and everything about it, and you're a nut for the complicated dance of perfect timing and arrangement of tones. At the very least, we assume that you have a couple of books of sheet music lying around that have been frustrating you, or you have an old piano in the corner of your house that you'd like to mess around with.

This book is written for the following types of musicians (which, frankly, covers the gamut):

✔ **The absolute beginner:** We wrote this book with the intent that it would accompany the beginning musician from his very first steps into note reading and tapping out rhythms all the way into his first real attempts at composing music by using the principles of music theory. Beginning musicians should start with Part I at the beginning of the book and just keep reading until reaching the back cover. The book is organized to follow the lesson plan that college music theory classes offer.

✔ **The music student who drifted away:** This book can also be helpful for the musician who took instrument lessons as a child and still remembers how to read sheet music but who was never exposed to the principles of building scales, following basic improvisation, or jamming with other musicians. Many folks fall into this camp, and, luckily, if you do, this book is designed to gently ease you back into the joy of playing music. It shows you how to work outside the constraints of playing from a piece of music and truly begin to improvise and even write your own music.

✔ **The experienced performer:** This book is also intended for the seasoned musician who already knows how to play music but never got around to working out how to read sheet music beyond the basic fakebook or lead sheet. If this description sounds like you, start with Part I, because it specifically discusses the note values used in sheet music. If you're already familiar with the concepts of eighth notes, quarter notes, and so on, Part II may be a good starting point. In that part of the book, we lay out the entire music staff and match it to both the piano keyboard and the guitar neck for easy reference.

Icons Used in This Book

Icons are handy little graphic images meant to point out particular types of information. You can find the following icons in this book; they're conveniently located along the left-hand margins.

This icon highlights time-saving advice and information that can help you understand key concepts.

When we discuss something that may be problematic or confusing, we use this icon.

This icon flags information that's, well, technical; you can go ahead and skip it if you want to.

When we make a point or offer some information that we feel you should keep with you forever, we toss in this icon.

This icon points out audio tracks that relate to the topic currently being discussed in the book. You can access the audio tracks at www.dummies. com/musictheory.

Beyond the Book

There's a lot of supplemental material for the book that can be found at www.dummies.com/extras/musictheory. You can check out many musical examples, quick reference material that is perfect for printing and shoving in your back pocket or guitar case to take with you to class, and interesting factoids about music in general.

Where to Go from Here

If you're a beginning music student or want to start again fresh, plow through Part I. If you're already familiar with the basics of rhythm and want to simply find out how to read notes, head to Part II. If you're a trained musician who wants to know how to improvise and begin to write music, Part III covers the basics of chord progressions, scales, and cadences. You can also check out Part IV, which discusses a variety of musical forms you can start plugging your own musical ideas into.

Relax and have fun with your quest into music theory. Listening to, playing, and writing music are some of the most enjoyable experiences you'll ever have. *Music Theory For Dummies,* 3rd Edition, may have been written by teachers, but we promise, no clock-watching tyrants will show up at your door to see how fast you're making your way through this book! We hope you enjoy reading this book as much as we did writing it. Sit back, read, and then start your own musical adventure.

Part I

Getting Started with Music Theory

In this part . . .

- ✔ Get to know music theory basics.
- ✔ Understand notes and rests.
- ✔ Read time signatures.
- ✔ Figure out beat patterns and rhythms.

Chapter 1

What Is Music Theory, Anyway?

* *

In This Chapter

▶ Checking out a bit of music history

▶ Getting to know the basics of music theory

▶ Finding out how theory can affect your playing

* *

*O*ne of the most important things to remember about music theory is that music came first. Music existed for thousands of years before theory came along to explain what people were trying to accomplish when pounding on their drums. So don't ever think that you can't be a good musician just because you've never taken a theory class. In fact, if you are a good musician, you likely already know a lot of theory. You simply may not know the terminology or technicalities.

The concepts and rules that make up music theory are much like the grammatical rules that govern written language (which also came along after people had successfully discovered how to talk to one another). Just as being able to transcribe language made it possible for people far away to "hear" conversations and stories the way the author intended, being able to transcribe music allows musicians to read and play compositions exactly as the composer intended. Learning to read music is a lot like learning a new language, to the point where a fluent person can "hear" a musical "conversation" when reading a piece of sheet music.

Plenty of people in the world can't read or write, but they can still communicate their thoughts and feelings verbally just fine. In the same way, plenty of intuitive, self-taught musicians have never learned to read or write music and find the whole idea of learning music theory tedious and unnecessary. However, just like the educational leaps that can come with learning to read and write, music theory can help musicians master new techniques, perform unfamiliar styles of music, and develop the confidence they need to try new things.

Unearthing Music Theory's Beginnings

From what historians can tell, by the time the ancient world was beginning to establish itself — approximately 7000 B.C. — musical instruments had already achieved a complexity in design that would be carried all the way into the present. For example, some of the bone flutes found from this time period are still playable, and short performances have been recorded on them for modern listeners to hear.

Similarly, pictographs and funerary ornaments have shown that by 3500 B.C., Egyptians were using harps as well as double-reed clarinets, lyres, and their own version of the flute. By 1500 B.C., the Hittites of northern Syria had modified the traditional Egyptian lute/harp design and invented the first two-stringed guitar, with a long, fretted neck, tuning pegs at the top of the neck, and a hollow soundboard to amplify the sound of the strings being plucked.

A lot of unanswered questions remain about ancient music, such as why so many different cultures came up with so many of the same tonal qualities in their music completely independent of one another. Many theorists have concluded that certain patterns of notes just sound right to listeners, and certain other patterns don't. Music theory, then, very simply, could be defined as a search for how and why music sounds right or wrong. In other words, the purpose of music theory is to explain *why* something sounded the way it did and *how* that sound can be made again.

Many people consider ancient Greece to be the actual birthplace of music theory, because the ancient Greeks started entire schools of philosophy and science built around dissecting every aspect of music that was known then. Even Pythagoras (the triangle guy) got into the act by creating the 12-pitch octave scale similar to the one that musicians and composers still use today (see Chapter 7). He did this via the first Circle of Fifths (see Chapter 8), a device still religiously used by musicians from all walks of life.

Another famous Greek scientist and philosopher, Aristotle, is responsible for many books about music theory. He began a rudimentary form of music notation that remained in use in Greece and subsequent cultures for nearly a thousand years after his death.

In fact, so much music theory groundwork was laid in ancient Greece that substantial changes didn't seem necessary until the European Renaissance nearly 2,000 years later. Neighbors and conquerors of Greece were all more than happy to incorporate Greek math, science, philosophy, art, literature, and music into their own cultures.

Putting the Spotlight on Music Theory Fundamentals

While it would be nice to be one of those people who can sit at any instrument and play beautiful music without any training whatsoever, most folks need some sort of structured instruction, whether from a teacher or from reading a book. In the following sections, we go over the basic information you need to start learning how to read music, play scales, understand key signatures, build chords, and compose with forms.

Understanding the foundation: Notes, rests, and beats

Learning how to read music is essential to a musician, especially one who wants to share his music with other musicians or discover what other musicians are playing. By studying the basic elements, such as time values of each type of written note (see Chapter 2), musical rests (see Chapter 3), time signatures (see Chapter 4), and rhythm (see Chapter 5), you put yourself on the path to mastering music. All these elements come together to establish a foundation that allows you to read, play, and study music.

Manipulating and combining notes

Reading musical notes on both the treble and bass clef staves as well as finding notes on the piano and guitar — the two most common instruments on which people teach themselves to play — are crucial to making and studying music. Chapter 6 gives you the full scoop.

When you can read notes on the staves, you can determine a musical piece's *key signature*, which is a group of symbols that tells you what key that song is written in. You can use the Circle of Fifths to help train yourself to read key signatures on sight by counting the sharps or flats in a time signature. You can read more about key signatures and the Circle of Fifths in Chapter 8.

After you've become familiar with key signatures, you're ready to move on to intervals, chords, and chord progressions, which create the complexity of musical sound — from pleasing and soothing to tense and in need of resolution. As we discuss in Chapter 9, you build scales and chords using simple or compound intervals: melodic and harmonic. Chapters 10 and 11 show you everything you need to know about building chords and chord progression, as well as how to build and use extended chords.

Linking the keyboard to music notation

Prior to the Renaissance period, few truly innovative changes occurred in music technology. Stringed instruments, woodwinds, horns, and percussion instruments had been around for thousands of years, and although they had experienced many improvements in design and playing technique, they were essentially the same instruments used by the people of ancient cultures. It wasn't until the 1300s that a brand new musical interface appeared: the keyboard.

With the invention of the keyboard came the beginning of modern musical notation — written music. The keyboard-notation link was fostered because of the ease of composing for full orchestras on the keyboard. Also, most newly commissioned work was created for keyboard instruments because of the public's perception of the keyboard as a superior instrument.

Fifteenth-century French composers began adding as many lines as they needed to their musical staves (see Chapter 6 to find out about the musical staff). They also wrote music with multiple staves to be played simultaneously by different instruments. Because the keyboard has so many notes available, separate staves for left- and right-handed playing began to be used. These staves are the bass clef and the treble clef.

As noted in Chapter 10, keyboards also had the advantage of being incredibly easy to build chords on. By the 17th century, the five-lined staff was considered standard for most musical instrumentation — probably because it was easier and cheaper to print just one kind of sheet music for musicians to compose on. The system hasn't changed much over the past four centuries, and it probably won't change again until a new, more-appealing instrument interface enters the scene.

Studying musical form and compositions

Most popular and classical music is composed using specific forms. A *form* is a structural blueprint used to create a certain type of music. The building blocks of form include musical phrases and periods (which we cover in Chapter 14), and rhythm, melody, and harmony enter the picture to create the *genre*, or style, of a piece of music.

When sitting down to write music, you have to choose what form you're going to follow; for example, classical or popular. You can choose from many different classical and popular forms, including sonatas, concertos, 16-bar blues, and verse-chorus form (Chapters 15 and 16 provide plenty of information on the forms you may encounter). You can create varied sound in whatever form you choose by playing with tempo, dynamics, and instrument tone color (see Chapters 12 and 13 for more).

Seeing How Theory Can Help Your Music

If you didn't know better, you may think that music was something that could start on any note, go wherever it wanted, and stop whenever the performer felt like getting up for a glass of iced tea. Although it's true that many folks have been to musical performances that actually do follow this style of "composition," for the most part these performances are confusing and annoyingly self-indulgent and feel a little pointless.

The only people who can pull off a spontaneous jam *well* are those who know music thoroughly enough to stack chords and notes next to one another so they make sense to listeners. And, because music is inherently a form of communication, connecting with your listeners is the goal.

Getting to know more about music theory is also incredibly inspiring. Nothing can describe the feeling you get when the light bulb goes off in your head and you suddenly realize you can put a 12-bar blues progression together and build a really good song out of it. Or when you can look at a piece of classical music and find yourself looking forward to playing through it for the first time. Or the first time you sit down to jam with your friends and find you have the confidence to take the lead.

As a musician, the inescapable fact is this: What you get out of music is what you put into it. If you want to be able to play classical music, you must know how to sight-read and know how to keep a steady beat. If you plan to become a rock guitarist, knowing what notes you need to play in a given key is especially important. Knowing how to play music takes a lot of personal discipline, but in the end, it's worth all the hard work. Plus, of course, playing music is fun, and knowing how to play music well is incredibly fun. Everybody loves a rock star/jazz man/Mozart.

Chapter 2

Determining What Notes Are Worth

*J*ust about everyone has taken some sort of music lessons, either formal paid lessons from a local piano teacher or at the very least the state-mandated rudimentary music classes offered in public school. Either way, we're sure you've been asked at some point to knock out a beat, if only by clapping your hands.

Maybe the music lesson seemed pretty pointless at the time or served only as a great excuse to bop your grade-school neighbor on the head. However, counting out a beat is exactly where you have to start with music. Without a discernible beat, you have nothing to dance or nod your head to. Although all the other parts of music (pitch, melody, harmony, and so on) are pretty darned important, without the beat, you don't really have a song.

Everything around you has a rhythm to it, including you. In music, the *rhythm* is the pattern of regular or irregular pulses. The most basic thing you're striving to find in songs is the rhythm. Luckily, written music makes it easy to interpret other composers' works and produce the kind of rhythm they had in mind for their songs.

In this chapter, we provide you with a solid introduction to the basics of counting notes and discovering a song's rhythm, beat, and tempo.

Note: You may notice in this chapter that we've given two different names for the notes mentioned — for example, quarter (crotchet) note. The first name (quarter) is the common U.S. name for the note, and the second name (crotchet) is the common U.K. name for the same note. The U.K. names are also used in medieval music and in some classical circles. After Chapter 3, we use only the U.S. common names for the notes, because the U.S. usage is more universally standard.

Meeting the Beat

A *beat* is a pulsation that divides time into equal lengths. A ticking clock is a good example. Every minute, the second hand ticks 60 times, and each one of those ticks is a beat. If you speed up or slow down the second hand, you're changing the *tempo* of the beat. *Notes* in music tell you what to play during each of those ticks. In other words, the notes tell you how long and how often to play a certain musical *pitch* — the low or high sound a specific note makes — within the beat.

When you think of the word *note* as associated with music, you may think of a sound. However, in music, one of the main uses for notes is to explain exactly how long a specific pitch should be held by the voice or an instrument. The *note value,* indicated by the size and shape of the note, determines this length. Together with the preceding three features, the note value determines what kind of rhythm the resulting piece of music has. It determines whether the song runs along very quickly and cheerfully, crawls along slowly and somberly, or progresses in some other way.

When figuring out how to follow the beat, *rhythm sticks* (fat, cylindrical, hard-wood instruments) come in real handy. So do drum sticks. If you've got a pair, grab 'em. If you don't, clapping or smacking your hand against bongos or your desktop works just as well.

Eventually "hearing" a beat in your head (or "feeling" a beat in your body) is absolutely fundamental while you play music, whether you're reading a piece of sheet music or jamming with other musicians. The only way you can master this basic task is *practice, practice, practice.* Following along with the beat is something you need to pick up if you want to progress in music.

Perhaps the easiest way to practice working with a steady beat is to buy a metronome. They're pretty cheap (you may even be able to find an app for your smartphone). Even a crummy metronome should last you for years. The beauty of a metronome is that you can set it to a wide range of tempos, from very, very slow to hummingbird fast. If you're using a metronome to practice — especially if you're reading from a piece of sheet music — you can set the beat to whatever speed you're comfortable with and gradually speed it up to the composer's intended speed when you've figured out the pacing of the song.

Recognizing Notes and Note Values

If you think of music as a language, then notes are like letters of the alphabet — they're that basic to the construction of a piece of music. Studying how note values fit against each other in a piece of sheet music is as important as knowing musical pitches because if you change the note values, you end up with completely different music. In fact, when musicians talk about performing a piece of music "in the style of" Bach, Beethoven, or Philip Glass, they're talking as much about using the rhythm structure and pace characteristics of that particular composer's music as much as any particular chord progressions or melodic choices.

In this section, we take a closer look at notes and what they're made of. We also discuss the basics on note values. For more in-depth info on notes, check out Chapter 6.

Examining the notes and their components

Notes are made of up to three specific components: note head, stem, and flag (see Figure 2-1).

- ✔ **Head:** The *head* is the round part of a note. Every note has one.
- ✔ **Stem:** The *stem* is the vertical line attached to the note head. Eighth (quaver) notes, quarter (crotchet) notes, and half (minim) notes all have stems.
- ✔ **Flag:** The *flag* is the little line that comes off the top or bottom of the note stem. Eighth (quaver) notes and shorter notes have flags.

Stems can point either up or down, depending where on the *staff* they appear (you find out all about staves in Chapters 4 and 6). Whether the stem points up or down makes no difference in the value of the note.

Figure 2-1:
The whole (semibreve) note has a head; the quarter (crotchet) note has a head and stem; and the eighth (quaver) note has a head, stem, and flag.

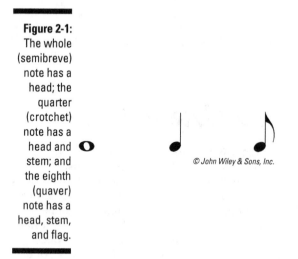

Instead of each note getting a flag, notes with flags can also be connected to each other with a *beam,* which is just a cleaner-looking incarnation of the flag. For example, Figure 2-2 shows how two eighth (quaver) notes can be written as each having a flag, or as connected by a beam.

Figure 2-2:
You can write eighth (quaver) notes with individual flags, or you can connect them with a beam.

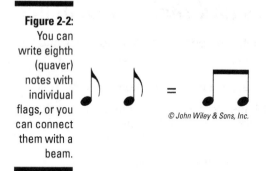

Figure 2-3 shows four sixteenth (semiquaver) notes with flags grouped three separate ways: individually, in two pairs connected by a double beam, and all connected by one double beam. It doesn't matter which way you write them; they sound the same when played.

Figure 2-3:
These three groups of sixteenth (semiquaver) notes, written in three different ways, all sound alike when played.

Likewise, you can write eight thirty-second (demisemiquaver) notes in either of the ways shown in Figure 2-4. Notice that these notes get *three* flags (or three beams). Using beams instead of individual flags on notes is simply a case of trying to clean up an otherwise messy-looking piece of musical notation. Beams help musical performers by allowing them to see where the larger beats are. Instead of seeing sixteen disconnected sixteenth (semiquaver) notes, it's helpful for a performer to see four groups of four sixteenths (semiquavers) connected by a beam.

Figure 2-4:
Like eighth (quaver) notes and sixteenth (semiquaver) notes, you can write thirty-second (demisemiquaver) notes separately or "beamed" together.

Looking at note values

As you may remember from school or music lessons, each note has its own note *value.* We go into detail on each kind of note later in this chapter, but for now, have a look at Figure 2-5, which shows most of the kinds of notes you'll encounter in music arranged so their values add up the same in each row. At the top is the whole (semibreve) note, below that half (minim) notes, then quarter (crotchet) notes, eighth (quaver) notes, and finally sixteenth (semiquaver) notes on the bottom. Each level of the "tree of notes" is equal to the others. The value of a half (minim) note, for example, is half of a whole (semibreve) note, and the value of a quarter (crotchet) note is a quarter of a whole (semibreve) note.

Figure 2-5:
Each level
of this tree
of notes
lasts as
many beats
as every
other level.

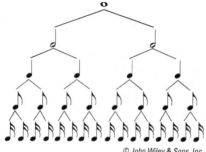

© John Wiley & Sons, Inc.

 Another way to think of notes is to imagine a whole (semibreve) note as a pie, which is easy because it's round. To divvy up the pie into quarter (crotchet) notes, cut it in quarters. Cutting the pie into eight pieces gives you eighth (quaver) notes, and so on.

Depending on the time signature of the piece of music (see Chapter 4), the note value that's equal to one beat changes. In the most common time signature, 4/4 time, also called *common time,* a whole (semibreve) note is held for four beats, a half (minim) note is held for two, and a quarter (crotchet) note lasts one beat. An eighth (quaver) note lasts half a beat, and a sixteenth (semiquaver) note lasts just a quarter of a beat in 4/4 time.

 Often, the quarter (crotchet) note equals one beat. If you sing, "MA-RY HAD A LIT-TLE LA-MB," each syllable is one beat (you can clap along with it), and each beat gets one quarter (crotchet) note if the song is notated in 4/4 time. We talk more about time signatures and counting beats accordingly in Chapter 4.

Checking Out Whole (Semibreve) Notes

The whole note (called a *semibreve* note in the U.K.) lasts the longest of all the notes. Figure 2-6 shows what it looks like.

Figure 2-6:
A whole (semibreve) note is a hollow oval.

© John Wiley & Sons, Inc.

In 4/4 time, a whole (semibreve) note lasts for an entire four beats (see Chapter 4 for more on time signatures). For four whole beats (semibreves), you don't have to do anything with that one note except play and hold it. That's it.

Usually, when you count note values, you clap or tap on the note and say aloud the remaining beats. You count the beats of whole (semibreve) notes like the ones shown in Figure 2-7, like this:

CLAP two three four CLAP two three four CLAP two three four

"CLAP" means you clap your hands, and "two three four" is what you say out loud as the note is held for four beats, or a four-count.

Figure 2-7:
When you see three whole (semibreve) notes in a row, each one gets its own "four-count."

© John Wiley & Sons, Inc.

Even better for the worn-out musician is coming across a double whole (breve) note. You don't see them a whole heck of a lot, but when you do, they look like Figure 2-8, and they're generally used in slow-moving processional music or in medieval music. When you see a double whole (breve) note, you have to hold the note for an entire eight counts, like so:

CLAP two three four five six seven eight

Figure 2-8:
Hold a
double
whole
(breve) note
for eight
counts.

© John Wiley & Sons, Inc.

You can also show a note that lasts for eight counts by tying together two whole (semibreve) notes. We discuss *ties* later in this chapter.

Homing In on Half (Minim) Notes

It's simple logic what comes after whole (semibreve) notes in value — a half (minim) note, of course. You hold a half (minim) note for half as long as you would a whole (semibreve) note. Half (minim) notes look like the notes in Figure 2-9. When you count out the half (minim) notes in Figure 2-9, it sounds like this:

CLAP two CLAP two CLAP two

Because the highest-valued note in Figure 2-9 is a half (minim) note, you count up only to the number two.

Figure 2-9:
Hold a half
(minim) note
for half as
long as a
whole (semi-
breve) note.

© John Wiley & Sons, Inc.

You could have a whole (semibreve) note followed by two half (minim) notes, as shown in Figure 2-10. In that case, you count out the three notes as follows:

CLAP two three four CLAP two CLAP two

Figure 2-10:
A whole
(semibreve)
note
followed
by two half
(minim)
notes.

© John Wiley & Sons, Inc.

Considering Quarter (Crotchet) Notes

Divide a whole (semibreve) note, which is worth four beats, by four, and you get a quarter (crotchet) note with a note value of one beat. Quarter (crotchet) notes look like half (minim) notes except that the note head is completely filled in, as shown in Figure 2-11. Four quarter (crotchet) notes are counted out like this:

CLAP CLAP CLAP CLAP

Because the highest-valued note is a quarter (crotchet) note, you count up only to one. Four quarter (crotchet) notes together last as long as one whole (semibreve) note.

Figure 2-11:
These four
quarter
(crotchet)
notes get
one beat
apiece.

© John Wiley & Sons, Inc.

Suppose you replace one of the quarter (crotchet) notes with a whole (semibreve) note and one with a half (minim) note, as shown in Figure 2-12. In that case, you count out the notes like this:

CLAP two three four CLAP CLAP CLAP two

Figure 2-12:
A mixture of whole (semibreve), half (minim), and quarter (crotchet) notes is getting closer to what you find in music.

© John Wiley & Sons, Inc.

Examining Eighth (Quaver) Notes and Beyond

When sheet music includes eighth (quaver) notes and beyond, it really starts to look a little intimidating. Usually, just one or two clusters of eighth (quaver) notes in a piece of musical notation isn't enough to frighten the average beginning student, but when that same student opens to a page that's littered with eighth (quaver) notes, sixteenth (semiquaver) notes, or thirty-second (demisemiquaver) notes, she just knows she has some work ahead of her. Why? Because usually these notes are *fast*.

An eighth (quaver) note, shown in Figure 2-13, has a value of half a quarter (crotchet) note. Eight eighth (quaver) notes last as long as one whole (semibreve) note, which means an eighth (quaver) note lasts half a beat (in 4/4, or common, time).

Figure 2-13:
You hold an eighth (quaver) note for one-eighth as long as a whole (semibreve) note.

© John Wiley & Sons, Inc.

How can you have half a beat? Easy. Tap your toe for the beat and clap your hands twice for every toe tap.

CLAP-CLAP CLAP-CLAP CLAP-CLAP CLAP-CLAP

Or you can count it out as follows:

ONE-and TWO-and THREE-and FOUR-and

The numbers represent four beats, and the "ands" are the half beats.

Just think of each tick of a metronome as an eighth (quaver) note instead of a quarter (crotchet) note. That means a quarter (quaver) note is now two ticks, a half (minim) note is four ticks, and a whole (semibreve) note lasts eight ticks.

Similarly, if you have a piece of sheet music with sixteenth (semiquaver) notes, each sixteenth (semiquaver) note can equal one metronome tick, an eighth (quaver) note two ticks, a quarter (crotchet) note four ticks, a half (minim) note eight ticks, and a whole (semibreve) note can equal sixteen ticks.

A sixteenth (semiquaver) note has a note value of one quarter of a quarter (crotchet) note, which means it lasts one-sixteenth as long as a whole (semibreve) note. A sixteenth (semiquaver) note looks like the note in Figure 2-14.

If you have a piece of sheet music with thirty-second (demisemiquaver) notes, as shown in Figure 2-15, remember that a thirty-second (demisemi-quaver) note equals one metronome tick, a sixteenth (semiquaver) note equals two, an eighth (quaver) note equals four, a quarter (crotchet) note equals eight, a half (minim) note equals sixteen, and a whole (semibreve) note equals thirty-two ticks. You'll be glad to hear that you won't run into thirty-second (demisemiquaver) notes very often.

Figure 2-14:
You hold a sixteenth (semiqua-ver) note for half as long as an eighth (quaver) note.

© John Wiley & Sons, Inc.

Figure 2-15:
You hold a thirty-second (demisemi-quaver) note for half as long as a sixteenth (semiqua-ver) note.

© John Wiley & Sons, Inc.

Extending Notes with Dots and Ties

Sometimes you want to add to the value of a note. You have two main ways to extend a note's value in written music: *dots* and *ties.* We explain each in the following sections.

Using dots to increase a note's value

Occasionally, you come across a note followed by a small dot, called an *augmentation dot.* This dot indicates that the note's value is increased by one half of its original value. The most common use of the dotted note is when a half (minim) note is made to last three quarter (crotchet) note beats instead of two, as shown in Figure 2-16. Another way to think about dots is that they make a note equal to *three* of the next shorter value instead of two.

Figure 2-16:
You hold a dotted half (dotted minim) note for an additional one-half as long as a regular half (minim) note.

♩. = 3 beats

© John Wiley & Sons, Inc.

Less common, but still applicable here, is the dotted whole (dotted semibreve) note. This dotted note means the whole (semibreve) note's value is increased from four beats to six beats.

If you see two dots behind the note — called a *double-dotted note* — increase the time value of the note by another quarter of the original note, on top of the half increase indicated by the first dot. A half (minim) note with two dots behind it is worth two beats plus one beat plus one-half a beat, or three and a half beats. You rarely see this type of notation in modern music. Composer Richard Wagner was very fond of the triple-dotted note in the 1800s.

Adding notes together with ties

Another way to increase the value of a note is by *tying* it to another note, as Figure 2-17 shows. Ties connect notes of the same pitch together to create one sustained note instead of two separate ones. When you see a tie, simply add the notes together. For example, a quarter (crotchet) note tied to another quarter (crotchet) note equals one note held for two beats:

CLAP-two!

Figure 2-17:
Two quarter (crotchet) notes tied together equal a half (minim) note.

© John Wiley & Sons, Inc.

Don't confuse ties with *slurs*. A slur looks kind of like a tie, except that it connects two notes of *different pitches*. (You find out more about slurs in Chapter 12.)

Mixing All the Note Values Together

You won't encounter many pieces of music that are composed entirely of one kind of note, so you need to practice working with a variety of note values.

The four exercises shown in Figures 2-18 through 2-21 can help make a beat stick in your head and make each kind of note automatically register its value in your brain. Each exercise contains five groups (or *measures*) of four beats each. The measures are notated with vertical lines, called *bar lines,* which are explained more in Chapter 4.

In these exercises, you clap on the CLAPs and say the numbers aloud. Where you see a hyphenated CLAP-CLAP, do two claps per beat (in other words, two claps in the space of one normal clap).

To ease yourself into each exercise, start out counting and then dive in after you count four.

Exercise 1

CLAP CLAP CLAP CLAP | CLAP two three CLAP | CLAP two three four | CLAP two three four | CLAP CLAP CLAP four

Figure 2-18:
Exercise 1.

© John Wiley & Sons, Inc.

Exercise 2

CLAP two three four | CLAP two three four | CLAP CLAP three CLAP | CLAP two CLAP four | CLAP two three four

Figure 2-19:
Exercise 2.

© John Wiley & Sons, Inc.

Exercise 3

CLAP CLAP-CLAP CLAP four | CLAP two three four | CLAP two three
CLAP | CLAP-CLAP CLAP three four | CLAP two CLAP four

Figure 2-20:
Exercise 3.

Exercise 4

CLAP two CLAP four | CLAP two three CLAP | CLAP two three four | one
CLAP three four | CLAP two three four

Figure 2-21:
Exercise 4.

Chapter 3

Giving It a Rest

Sometimes the most important aspects of a conversation are the things that aren't said. Likewise, many times the notes you don't play make all the difference in a piece of music.

These silent "notes" are called, quite fittingly, *rests*. When you see a rest in a piece of music, you don't have to do anything but continue counting out the beats during it. Rests are especially important when writing down your music for other people to read — and in reading other composers' music — because rests make the rhythm of that piece of music even more precise than musical notes alone would.

Rests work particularly well with music for multiple instruments. Rests make it easy for a performer to count out the beats and keep time with the rest of the ensemble, even if the performer's instrument doesn't come into play until later in the performance. Likewise, in piano music, rests tell the left or right hand — or both — to stop playing in a piece.

Don't let the name fool you. A rest in a piece of music is anything but nap time. If you don't continue to steadily count through the rests, just as you do when you're playing notes, your timing will be off, and eventually the piece will fall apart.

Note: You may notice in this chapter that we've given two different names for the notes or rests mentioned — for example, quarter (crotchet) rest. The first name (quarter) is the common U.S. name for the rest, and the second name (crotchet) is the common U.K. name for the same rest. The U.K. names are also used in medieval music and in some classical circles. After this chapter, we only use the U.S. names for notes and rests, because the U.S. usage is more globally recognized.

Getting to Know the Rests

Think of rests as the spaces between words in a written sentence. If those spaces weren't there, you'd just be stringing one long word together into gobbledygook.

Musical rests don't get claps (or notes from instruments or voices). You just count them out in your head. Just remember to stop playing your instrument while you're counting.

Figure 3-1 shows the relative values of rests, ranging from a whole (semibreve) rest at the top to the sixteenth (semiquaver) rests at the bottom. At the top is the whole (semibreve) rest, below it half (minim) rests, then quarter (crotchet) rests, eighth (quaver) rests, and sixteenth (semiquaver) rests. We discuss each of these rests in the following sections.

Figure 3-1:
Each level
of this tree
of rests
lasts as
many beats
as every
other level.

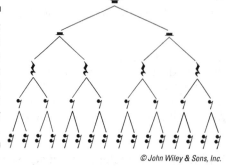

© John Wiley & Sons, Inc.

Whole (semibreve) rests

Just like a whole (semibreve) note, a whole (semibreve) rest is worth four beats (in the most common time signature, 4/4; see Chapter 4 for all you need to know about time signatures). Look at Figure 3-2 for an example of a whole (semibreve) rest.

The whole (semibreve) rest looks like an upside-down hat. You can remember what this rest looks like by imagining it's a hat that has been taken off and set down on a table, because this rest is a long one.

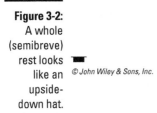

Figure 3-2:
A whole (semibreve) rest looks like an upside-down hat.

© John Wiley & Sons, Inc.

Even better than a double whole (breve) note for the worn-out musician is the very rare double whole (breve) rest, which you can see in Figure 3-3. When you come across one of these, usually in 4/2 music, you don't have to play anything for eight beats.

Figure 3-3:
You'll rarely encounter the double whole (breve) rest.

© John Wiley & Sons, Inc.

Half (minim) rests

If a whole (semibreve) rest is held for four beats, then a half (minim) rest is held for two beats. Half (minim) rests look like the one in Figure 3-4.

Figure 3-4:
The half (minim) rest lasts half as long as the whole (semibreve) rest.

© John Wiley & Sons, Inc.

As do whole (semibreve) rests, half (minim) rests also look like hats. However, the half (minim) rest is right side up because the wearer didn't have time to lay it down on a table.

Take a look at the notes and rest in Figure 3-5. If you were to count out this music in 4/4 time, it would sound like this:

CLAP two three four CLAP two REST two

Figure 3-5:
A whole (semibreve) note, half (minim) note, and half (minim) rest.

© John Wiley & Sons, Inc.

Quarter (crotchet) rests

Divide a whole (semibreve) rest by four or a half (minim) rest by two, and you get a quarter (crotchet) rest. A quarter (crotchet) rest, shown in Figure 3-6, lasts one-quarter as long as a whole (semibreve) rest.

Figure 3-6:
A quarter (crotchet) rest, written like a kind of squiggle, is like a silent quarter (crotchet) note.

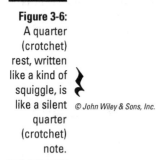

© John Wiley & Sons, Inc.

Figure 3-7 shows a whole (semibreve) note and a half (minim) note separated by two quarter (crotchet) rests. You would clap out the music in Figure 3-7 as follows:

CLAP two three four REST REST CLAP two

Figure 3-7:
Two quarter (crotchet) rests tucked between notes.

© John Wiley & Sons, Inc.

Eighth (quaver) rests and beyond

Eighth (quaver) rests, sixteenth (semiquaver) rests, and thirty-second (demisemiquaver) rests are easy to recognize because they all have little curlicue flags, a little bit like their note counterparts, as we explain in Chapter 2. Here's the lowdown on the different numbers of flags each note and rest has:

- ✔ **One flag:** Eighth (quaver) note and eighth (quaver) rest; see Figure 3-8.
- ✔ **Two flags:** Sixteenth (semiquaver) note and sixteenth (semiquaver) rest; see Figure 3-9.
- ✔ **Three flags:** Thirty-second (demisemiquaver) note and thirty-second (demisemiquaver) rest; see Figure 3-10.

Figure 3-8:
An eighth (quaver) rest has a stem and one curly flag.

© John Wiley & Sons, Inc.

As you may imagine, eighth (quaver) rests can be as tricky to count out as their note equivalents. An eighth (quaver) rest lasts half as long as a quarter (crotchet) rest, which usually means less than a whole beat. Eight eighth (quaver) rests make up a whole (semibreve) rest.

Using a metronome to count out notes and rests may help you figure out a piece of music. You can assign the ticks of the metronome to be any portion of the beat that you want. Having a quarter (crotchet) note equal one beat may seem natural much of the time, but instead of trying to think about half beats, you can also assign an eighth (quaver) note to equal one tick. Then a quarter (crotchet) note would equal two ticks, a half (minim) note four, and a whole (semibreve) note eight ticks. The relation among the different notes and rests always stays the same no matter how many metronome ticks in a whole (semibreve) note.

A sixteenth (semiquaver) rest looks like the one in Figure 3-9. It has a note value of one-sixteenth of a whole (semibreve) rest. In other words, sixteen sixteenth (semiquaver) rests make up a whole (semibreve) rest.

Figure 3-9:
A sixteenth (semiqua-ver) rest has
two curly *© John Wiley & Sons, Inc.*
flags.

You probably won't ever encounter one, but you still need to be able to recognize a thirty-second (demisemiquaver) rest. A thirty-second (demisemi-quaver) rest, which is shown in Figure 3-10, has a value of one thirty-second of a whole (semibreve) rest. So thirty-two thirty-second (demisemiquaver) rests make up a whole (semibreve) rest.

Figure 3-10:
A thirty-second (demisemi-quaver) rest
is very rare
and has *© John Wiley & Sons, Inc.*
three curly
flags.

Extending the Break with Dotted Rests

Unlike notes, rests are never tied together to make them longer. Rests are, however, sometimes dotted when the value of the rest needs to be extended. Just like with notes, when you see a rest followed by an *augmentation dot*, the rest's value is increased by one half of its original value. (Flip to Chapter 2 for details on dots and ties.)

Figure 3-11 shows a dotted half (minim) rest, which you hold for a half (minim) rest plus one-half of a half (minim) rest. A dotted quarter (crotchet) rest is extended by another half of a quarter (crotchet) rest.

Figure 3-11:
Hold a dotted half (minim) rest for a half (minim) rest plus one-half of a half (minim) rest, making it worth three quarter (crotchet) rests.

© John Wiley & Sons, Inc.

Practicing Beats with Notes and Rests

The best way to really hear the way rests affect a piece of music is to mix them up with notes. To avoid adding to the confusion, we use only quarter (crotchet) notes in the following exercises.

The five exercises shown in Figures 3-12 through 3-16 are exactly what you need to practice making a beat stick in your head and making each kind of note and rest automatically register its value in your brain. Each exercise contains three groups of four beats each.

In these exercises, with four beats in every measure (4/4 time), you clap on the notes and count the rests aloud. Start out counting and then dive in after you count four.

Exercise 1

CLAP CLAP CLAP CLAP | One two three four | CLAP two three CLAP

Figure 3-12:
Exercise 1.

Exercise 2

One two three four | CLAP two CLAP four | CLAP two three CLAP

Figure 3-13:
Exercise 2.

Exercise 3

One CLAP three CLAP | One two three four | CLAP two three CLAP

Figure 3-14:
Exercise 3.

Exercise 4

One two CLAP CLAP | One two three four | CLAP CLAP CLAP four

Figure 3-15:
Exercise 4.

© John Wiley & Sons, Inc.

Exercise 5

One two three four | CLAP two three CLAP | One two CLAP
CLAP

Figure 3-16:
Exercise 5.

© John Wiley & Sons, Inc.

Chapter 4

Introducing Time Signatures

In This Chapter

▷ Discovering measures and time signatures

▷ Knowing the difference between simple and compound time signatures

▷ Finding out about asymmetrical time signatures

*I*f you're worried about how you're supposed to keep track of where you are in a long piece of music, never fear. The geniuses who came up with music notation figured out a way to make order of the onslaught of notes and rests. You just have to become familiar with time signatures and the structure of the musical staff, including the concept of measures (or bars). This chapter explains everything you need to know.

Decoding Time Signatures and Measures

In printed music, right after the clef and the key signature (see Chapter 8 for more about key signatures) at the beginning of the staff, you see a pair of numbers, one written over the other.

The pair of numbers is called the *time signature*, which, incidentally, is the main topic of this chapter. The time signature tells you two things:

✔ **The number of beats in each measure:** The top number in the time signature tells you the number of beats to be counted off in each measure. If the top number is three, each measure contains three beats.

✔ **Which note gets one beat:** The bottom number in the time signature tells you which type of note value equals one beat — most often, eighth notes and quarter notes. If the bottom number is four, a quarter note is one beat. If it's an eight, an eighth note carries the beat.

Figure 4-1 shows three common time signatures.

Written music contains the following two main types of time signatures, which we cover later in this chapter:

✔ **Simple:** With simple time signatures, the beat of a piece of music can be broken down into two-part rhythms.

✔ **Compound:** In compound time signatures, the beat is broken down into three-part rhythms.

A *measure* (sometimes called a *bar*) is a segment of written music contained within two vertical lines. Each measure in a piece of music has as many beats as is allowed by the time signature. For instance, if you're working with a 4/4 time signature, each measure in that piece of music contains exactly four beats (as stated by the top number of the time signature) carried by notes or rests. If the time signature is 3/4, each measure has three beats in it, as shown in Figure 4-2. The one exception to this rule is when the measure uses pick-up notes (see Chapter 5 for more about pick-up notes). With these notes, you put a strong accent on the first beat of each measure, the "1" beat. Musicians call this the *downbeat*.

Figure 4-2:
Figure 4-2:
Given the 3/4
time signa-
ture, each
measure
contains
three beats,
and the
quarter note
equals one
beat.

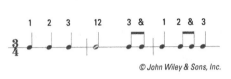

© John Wiley & Sons, Inc.

 Practicing counting through measures is a great way to make sure you're playing the piece of music in front of you according to the beat chosen by the composer. As we make clear in Chapters 2 and 3, continuously counting beats in your head while you're playing is incredibly important to the resulting sound. Timing is everything in music. You must become so comfortable with the inherent beat of whatever you're playing that you don't even know you're counting beats anymore.

Keeping Things Easy with Simple Time Signatures

Simple time signatures are the easiest to count, because a one-two pulse in a piece of music feels the most natural to a listener and a performer. The following four requirements indicate that a time signature is a simple one:

✔ **Each beat is divided into two equal components.** If a single beat has more than one note, those notes are always grouped together to equal one beat. This characteristic is most obvious when it's applied to eighth and smaller notes. In simple time, two eighth notes are always connected together with a bar called a *beam*, as are four sixteenth notes, or eight thirty-second notes. (If you have two sixteenth notes and one eighth note, those three notes, which equal one beat, are also beamed together.) Figure 4-3 shows the progression of how notes are beamed together in simple time.

✔ **The note that gets one beat has to be an undotted note.** When you're counting a song out in your head, you're going to be counting only undotted notes that are divisible by two. Usually this means you'll be counting quarter notes, but you also may be counting half notes, whole notes, or, sometimes, eighth notes.

In 4/4 time, for example, in your head you'll be counting, "One-two-three-four" over and over again. In 3/4 time, it'll be "one-two-three" over and over again; in 2/4 time, "one-two."

✔ **The top number isn't divisible by 3 except when it *is* 3.** For example, 3/4 and 3/8 are considered simple time signatures, whereas 6/4, 6/8, and 9/16 aren't (because they are divisible by 3; these are compound time signatures).

✔ **The number of beats is the same in every measure.** Every measure, or bar, of music in a simple time signature has the same number of beats throughout the song. After you get into the groove of counting out the time, you don't have to worry about doing anything but making sure the notes in the song follow that beat all the way through.

Figure 4-3:
Each level of this tree equals every other layer, and multiple notes within a beat are always grouped together to equal one beat.

© John Wiley & Sons, Inc.

The following sections explain how to use measures to count in simple time and provide you with some counting practice.

Using measures to count in simple time

Measures (or bars) help performers keep track of where they are in a piece of music and help them play the appropriate beat. In simple time, the measure is where the true rhythm of a piece of music can be felt, even if you're just reading a piece of sheet music without playing it.

In simple time, a slightly stronger accent is placed on the first beat of each measure.

Here are some common examples of simple time signatures (some of which we describe in the following sections):

- ✔ **4/4:** Used in popular, classical, rock, jazz, country, bluegrass, hip-hop, and house music
- ✔ **3/4:** Used for waltzes and country and western ballads
- ✔ **2/4:** Used in polkas and marches
- ✔ **3/8:** Used in waltzes, minuets, and country and western ballads
- ✔ **2/2:** Used in marches and slow-moving processionals

Counting 4/4 time

When you see a line of music that has a 4/4 time signature like the one in Figure 4-4, the beat is counted off like this:

ONE two three four ONE two three four ONE two three four

Figure 4-4:
A time signature of 4/4 satisfies the requirements of simple time.

© John Wiley & Sons, Inc.

The bottom number 4 in the time signature in Figure 4-4 tells you that the quarter note gets the beat, and the top number 4 tells you that each measure contains four beats, or four quarter notes.

Because 4/4 time is so often used in popular types of music, it's frequently referred to as *common time*. In fact, instead of writing "4/4" for the time signature, some composers just write a large "C" instead.

Counting 3/4 time

If the time signature of a line of music is 3/4, as in Figure 4-5, the beat is counted like this:

ONE two three ONE two three ONE two three

Figure 4-5:
A time
signature of
3/4 satisfies
the require-
ments of
simple time.

© John Wiley & Sons, Inc.

Counting 3/8 time

If the time signature is 3/8, the first note — whatever it may be — gets the beat. In Figure 4-6, that first note is an eighth note.

Figure 4-6:
A time
signature of
3/8 satisfies
the require-
ments of
simple time.

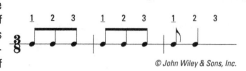

© John Wiley & Sons, Inc.

You count out the beat of the music shown in Figure 4-6 like this:

ONE two three ONE two three ONE two three

The time signatures 3/8 and 3/4 have almost exactly the same rhythm structure in the way the beat is counted off. However, because 3/8 uses eighth notes instead of quarter notes, the eighth notes get the beat.

Counting 2/2 time

If the time signature of a line is 2/2, also called *cut time*, the half note gets the beat. And because the top number determines that the measure contains two beats, you know that each measure has two half notes, as shown in Figure 4-7.

Figure 4-7:
In 2/2 time, the half note gets the beat, and each measure contains two beats.

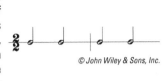

© John Wiley & Sons, Inc.

You count the music in Figure 4-7 like this:

ONE two ONE two

Time signatures with a 2 as the lower number were widely used in medieval and pre-medieval music. Music from this period used a rhythm structure, called a *tactus* — later called a *minim* — that was based on the rhythm pattern of a human heartbeat.

Practicing counting beats in simple time

Using the information from the preceding sections, practice counting out the *beats* (not the notes) shown in Figures 4-8 through 4-12. When counting these beats out loud, remember to give the first beat a slight stress. For a challenge, try tapping out the notes while you count the beats out loud.

Exercise 1

ONE two three four ❘ ONE two three four ❘ ONE two three four

Figure 4-8:
Exercise 1.

© John Wiley & Sons, Inc.

Exercise 2

ONE two three ❘ ONE two three ❘ ONE two three

Figure 4-9:
Exercise 2.

© John Wiley & Sons, Inc.

Exercise 3

ONE two three | ONE two three | ONE two three

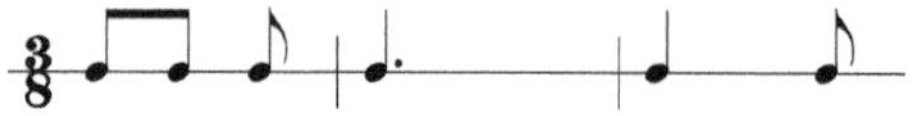

Figure 4-10:
Exercise 3.

© John Wiley & Sons, Inc.

Exercise 4

ONE two three | ONE two three | ONE two three

Figure 4-11:
Exercise 4.

© John Wiley & Sons, Inc.

Exercise 5

ONE two | ONE two | ONE two

Figure 4-12:
Exercise 5.

© John Wiley & Sons, Inc.

Working with Compound Time Signatures

Just a wee bit trickier than simple time signatures are *compound time signatures*. Here's a short list of rules that help you immediately tell when you're dealing with a compound time signature:

✔ **The top number is evenly divisible by 3, with the exception of time signatures where the top number is 3.** Any time signature with a top number of 6, 9, 12, 15, and so on according to the multiples of 3 is a compound time signature. However, 3/4 and 3/8 aren't compound time signatures because the top number is 3 (they're simple time signatures, which we discuss earlier). The most common compound time signatures are 6/8, 9/8, and 12/8. See Figure 4-13 for an example.

✔ **Each beat is divided into three components.** *Three* eighth notes are beamed together, as are *six* sixteenth notes. Figure 4-14 shows the "three-based" grouping of beamed notes used in compound time.

Figure 4-13:
A time signature of 6/8 is a compound time signature.

© John Wiley & Sons, Inc.

Figure 4-14:
Compound time divides notes into groups of three.

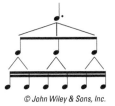

© John Wiley & Sons, Inc.

The following sections explain how to use measures to count in compound time and provide you with some counting practice.

Using measures to count in compound time

One big difference between music in a simple time signature and music in a compound time signature is that they *feel* different, both to listen to and to play.

In compound time, an accent is not only placed on the first beat of each measure (as in simple time), but a slightly softer accent is also placed on each successive beat. Therefore, there are two distinctly accented beats in each measure of music with a 6/8 time, three accents in a piece of 9/8 music, and four accents in a piece of music with a 12/8 time signature.

Here are a few examples of compound time signatures (some of which we cover in the following sections):

✔ **6/8:** Used in mariachi music

✔ **12/8:** Found in 12-bar blues and doo-wop music

✔ **9/4:** Used in jazz and progressive rock

To determine the number of accents per measure under a compound time signature, divide the top number by three. Doing so helps you find the pulse in the music you're playing and, therefore, where to put the accents. In a piece of 6/8 music, for example, you would put the accent at the beginning of each measure, but you also would put a slight accent at the beginning of the second group of eighth notes in a measure.

Counting 6/8 time

In a compound 6/8 time signature, you accent the first and the second sets of three eighth notes. For example, the beat accents in Figure 4-15 would go like this:

ONE two three FOUR five six ONE two three FOUR five six

Figure 4-15:
Accent the first and second sets of three eighth notes in a compound 6/8 time signature.

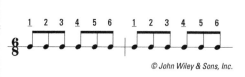

© John Wiley & Sons, Inc.

Counting 9/4 time

If the time signature is something unusual, like 9/4, an example of which is shown in Figure 4-16, you would count off the beat like so:

ONE two three FOUR five six SEVEN eight nine

Figure 4-16:
A time signature of 9/4 is a compound time signature.

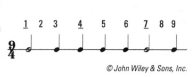

© John Wiley & Sons, Inc.

Practicing counting beats in compound time

Using the information from the preceding sections, practice counting out the beats in Figures 4-17 through 4-19. When counting these beats out loud, remember to give the first beat a slight stress and put an additional stress at the pulse points of the measure, which are generally located after every third beat. (***Note:*** The *and*s in the beat patterns are meant to capture the lilt of some of the notes within the beat. We admit this method isn't scientific, but it should give you a general idea of how to count out beats in different time signatures.)

Exercise 1

ONE two three FOUR-and five six | ONE two three FOUR five six | ONE two three FOUR five six

Figure 4-17:
Exercise 1.

© John Wiley & Sons, Inc.

Exercise 2

ONE two three FOUR-and-five-and-six-and | ONE two three FOUR five six | ONE two three FOUR-and-five-and-six-and

Figure 4-18:
Exercise 2.

© John Wiley & Sons, Inc.

Exercise 3

ONE two three FOUR five six SEVEN eight nine | ONE two three FOUR-and-five-and-six-and SEVEN eight nine

Figure 4-19:
Exercise 3.

© John Wiley & Sons, Inc.

Feeling the Pulse of Asymmetrical Time Signatures

Asymmetrical time signatures (also sometimes called *complex* or *irregular* time signatures) generally contain five or seven beats, compared to the traditional two-, three-, and four-beat measure groupings introduced earlier in this chapter (as part of simple and compound time signatures). Asymmetrical time signatures are common in traditional music from around the world, including in European folk music and in Eastern (particularly Indian) popular and folk music.

When you play or hear a piece of music with an asymmetrical time signature, you notice that the pulse of the song feels and sounds quite a bit different from music written under simple or compound time signatures. Music with 5/4, 5/8, and 5/16 time signatures is usually divided into two pulses — either two beats plus three beats, or vice versa. The stress pattern doesn't have to repeat itself from measure to measure; the only constant is that each measure still contains five beats.

For example, in Figure 4-20, the pulse is defined by the placements of the half notes in each grouping, making the stresses fall on the third beat in the first measure and on the fourth beat in the second measure, like this:

ONE two THREE four five | ONE two three FOUR five

Figure 4-20:
In this example of 5/4 time, the stress is on beats one, three, one, and four.

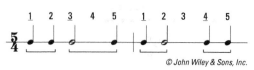

© John Wiley & Sons, Inc.

In Figure 4-21, the beaming of the eighth notes shows where the stresses are to occur — on the first eighth note of each set of beamed notes. Here's what it looks like if you say it out loud:

ONE two THREE four five | ONE two three FOUR five

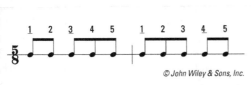

© John Wiley & Sons, Inc.

Music with 7/4, 7/8, and 7/16 time signatures looks like the music in Figures 4-22 and 4-23. Again, the stress patterns don't have to stay the same from one measure to the next.

If the time signature were 7/4, as shown in Figure 4-22, you would count off the beat like this:

ONE two three FOUR five six seven | ONE two three four FIVE six seven

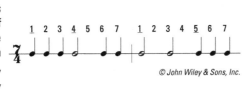

© John Wiley & Sons, Inc.

Here's how you count off a time signature of 7/8, as shown in Figure 4-23:

ONE two three FOUR five SIX seven | ONE two THREE four FIVE six seven

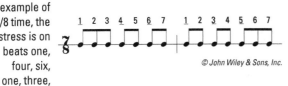

© John Wiley & Sons, Inc.

Asymmetrical time signatures are considered "complex" only from a Western point of view. These irregular time signatures have been used regularly throughout history and around the world, including in ancient Greece and Persia. They also can still be heard in Bulgarian folk music. Modern Western composers and ensembles as diverse as Steve Albini, Beck, Dave Brubeck, June of 44, Andrew Lloyd Webber, Frank Zappa, Pink Floyd, Yo-Yo Ma, Bobby McFerrin, and Stereolab have all used asymmetrical time signatures in their music. A whole genre of rock, called *math rock*, is based on using complex time signatures, such as 7/8, 11/8, 13/8, and so on, in order to break away from the 4/4 time that's the standard in rock.

Chapter 5

Playing with Beat

*T*he rules of notes and rests may seem strict, but even the most casual listener can recognize that music isn't a force controlled by robotic percussionists and gigantic clicking metronomes. If the world itself were a perfectly ordered organism, with every living thing on it moving along in perfect time, all music might sound similar. However, even the healthiest human heart skips a beat now and then, and so does music.

The trick for composers and music theorists alike has been to translate these skipped beats into written notation, making such deviations fit naturally into the score. This chapter explains everything you need to know about working with a beat.

Creating Stress Patterns and Syncopation

The underlying rhythmic pulse of music is called the *beat*. In some ways, the beat is everything. It determines how people dance to music or even how they feel when they hear it. The beat influences whether people feel excited, agitated, mellow, or relaxed by music. When you're writing a piece of music down on paper, the way you group your notes together in a *measure* (the music contained within two bar lines) reflects the kind of beat the music will have. As a musician, you can feel this natural pulse when you play music and count off the beats.

Placing stress: Knowing the general rules

Generally, the first beat of a measure receives the strongest stress. If more than three beats are in a measure, usually a secondary strong beat comes halfway through the measure. Lots of theories exist about why the brain seems to demand that music be broken up into units of two and three beats (not the least being that the beat of music tends to be similar to the beat of the human heart). But no one has come to a consensus on why music should be broken up into units of two or three beats.

In a piece of music with four beats in each measure, such as a piece in 4/4 time, the first beat in the measure has a strong accent, and the third beat has a slightly less strong accent. The beats would be counted as follows:

ONE two THREE four

A piece of music written in 6/8 time, which has six beats in each measure, is counted as follows:

ONE two three FOUR five six

See Chapter 4 for more on time signatures.

Syncopation: Hitting the off-beat

Syncopation is, very simply, a deliberate disruption of the two- or three-beat stress pattern. Musicians most often create syncopation by stressing an *off-beat*, or a note that isn't on the beat.

In 4/4 time, the general stress pattern is that the first and the third beats are strong, and the second and fourth are weak. Another way to say this is that *downbeats,* or accented beats, such as those at the beginning or halfway through a measure, are strong, and *upbeats*, or unaccented beats, are generally weak.

So if you had a piece of music that looked like the music in Figure 5-1, the quarter rest where the natural downbeat is located is considered the point of syncopation in the music. The fourth beat of the measure is accented instead of the third beat, which is normally accented, creating a different-sounding rhythm than you would normally have in 4/4 time music. The measure would be counted off as such:

ONE-two-three-FOUR

Figure 5-1:
A measure
with synco-
pation.

© John Wiley & Sons, Inc.

In Figure 5-1, the natural stress of the meter has been disrupted. The count
ONE-two-(three)-FOUR is weird to your ear because you want to hear that
nonexistent quarter note that would carry the downbeat in the middle of the
measure.

If you do anything that disrupts the natural beat with either an accent or an
upbeat with no subsequent downbeat being played, you have created
syncopation.

People often mistake syncopation as being comprised of cool, complex
rhythms with lots of sixteenth notes and eighth notes, as often heard in jazz
music, but that isn't necessarily true. For example, Figure 5-2 shows a bunch
of eighth notes and then a bunch of sixteenth and thirty-second notes.

Figure 5-2:
These mea-
sures may
look compli-
cated, but
they don't
show syn-
copation.

© John Wiley & Sons, Inc.

Just because Figure 5-2 shows a dense rhythm doesn't necessarily mean
those rhythms are syncopated. As you can see from the accent marks, the
downbeat is still on the "one" and "four" count in both measures, which is
the normal downbeat in 6/8 time.

Even if a piece of music contains an entire measure of eighth notes, it doesn't
necessarily have syncopation. Every eighth note has a subsequent *rhythmic
resolution.* In other words, the downbeats still occur in the measure where
they're supposed to be, on the accented notes shown in the figure. The
same is true of a bunch of sixteenth notes in a row. They aren't syncopated
because, again, even though you have some interesting notes that aren't on

the downbeat, everything ends up always resolving to the beat, like the following measure in 4/4 time:

ONE two THREE four

Here's another example of the beat resolving in 6/8 time:

ONE two three FOUR five six

Now take a look at the rhythm in Figure 5-3. Inside each box is a point of syncopation in the measures, giving you the following rhythm:

ONE two three FOUR one TWO three FOUR

The natural stresses have been shifted over in both measures, resulting in a purposefully disjointed-sounding beat.

Figure 5-3:
This music shows two places where the note placement creates syncopation.

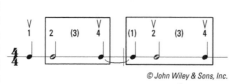

© John Wiley & Sons, Inc.

So does syncopation involve a carefully placed rest or an accented note? The answer is both. If your perspective of where the downbeat occurs is moved, a point of syncopation results because it's shifting where the strong and the weak accents are built.

Try counting out the beats while listening to the Rolling Stones' "Satisfaction," and you'll hear some great examples of syncopation.

Getting a Jump on Pick-Up Notes

Up until now, you've had to follow the rule that says 4/4 meter has four beats to every measure. Think of every measure like a jug of water that you have to fill right to the top without spilling over — you can't end up short and you can't spill any over. That's the rule.

But like every good rule, this one has an exception. It's called a *pick-up measure*, which is an odd measure at the beginning of a piece of music, as shown in Figure 5-4. This measure contains *pick-up notes*.

Figure 5-4:
The quarter note standing alone in the first measure is a pick-up note.

© John Wiley & Sons, Inc.

The pick-up measure shown in Figure 5-4 has only one beat where three should be (given that the piece is in 3/4 time). From that point on, the song follows the rules set forth by the 3/4 time signature all the way to the very end, where you suddenly come across a measure that looks like the one in Figure 5-5.

Figure 5-5:
The last measure of the song "picked up" the remaining two notes from the first incomplete pick-up measure.

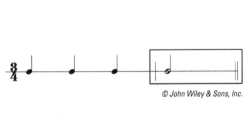

© John Wiley & Sons, Inc.

The final measure is the second part of the pick-up measure: The final two beats are considered the remainder part of the first measure. In other words, the last measure "fixes" what looked wrong with that first measure, and therefore you have a piece of music written according to all the rules of music theory.

Like a lot of cases when dealing with music theory, the matter of using pick-up notes is mostly notational. In Figure 5-5, the listener doesn't necessarily know that the last bar is incomplete unless she is listening really carefully. Usually, only the composer has to worry about the whole business of balancing out the end with the pick-up measure.

In contemporary music, especially rock music, you can still have the first pick-up measure, but you don't necessarily have to adhere to the perfect rule of finishing it in the final measure. Often musicians start a song with a pick-up measure, but their last measure is a complete one.

Exploring Irregular Rhythms: Triplets and Duplets

Another way you can add rhythmic interest and variety to music is through the use of irregular rhythms (also called *irrational rhythm* or *artificial division*). An *irregular rhythm* is any rhythm that involves dividing the beat differently from what's allowed by the time signature. The most common of these divisions is called a *triplet,* which is three notes joined together that equal the beat of a single note. The second most common type of irregular rhythm is a *duplet,* which is two bracketed notes with a note value of three of the same notes.

Irregular note divisions, such as triplets and duplets, allow for more complex rhythms than "regular" notation time normally allows.

The following sections dive deeper into triplets and duplets.

Adding interest with triplets

Say you want to put a quick little sequence of three notes where you'd normally play one quarter note. In 4/4 time, if you want to play an even number of notes in your sequence, you can use a couple of eighth notes, or four sixteenth notes, or eight thirty-second notes. But what if you want to play an odd number of notes, and you absolutely want that odd number of notes to equal one beat?

The answer is to play a *triplet,* which is what you get when you have a note that's usually divisible by two equal parts divided into three equal parts. You can see what a quarter note divided into triplets looks like in Figure 5-6.

A good way to count out the beats while playing triplets is to say the number of the beat followed by the word *triplet* (with two syllables), making sure to divide the triplet played into three equal parts.

Figure 5-6:
When a quarter note in 4/4 time is divided into three equal notes, the result is a triplet.

© John Wiley & Sons, In c.

For example, the measures in Figure 5-7 would be counted off like this:

ONE two THREE-trip-let four ONE-trip-let two THREE-trip-let four

Figure 5-7:
A piece of music using both quarter notes and triplets.

© John Wiley & Sons, Inc.

You can show the triplet notation in two ways: with the number 3 written over the group of three notes or with a bracket as well as the number. Read triplet notation as meaning "three notes in the time of two."

Working with duplets

Duplets work like triplets, except in reverse. Composers use duplets when they want to put two notes in a space where they should put three.

An example would be dividing a dotted quarter note into two eighth notes instead of three eighth notes as you would in a measure of music under a compound time signature (see Chapter 4 for more on compound time signatures). A good way to count duplets is to count the second note in each pair as *and* instead of assigning it a number value as you would any other beat in compound meter.

You count the measures shown in Figure 5-8 like this:

ONE two three FOUR-and ONE-and FOUR five six

© John Wiley & Sons, Inc.

Part II
Putting Notes Together

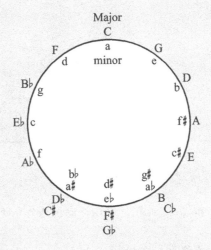

In this part . . .

- ✔ Discover the grand staff, treble and bass clefs, and note names.

- ✔ Get to know musical intervals, scales, and chords.

- ✔ Understand the Circle of Fifths and the relationship between keys and chords.

- ✔ Identify and create chords and chord progressions.

Chapter 6

Music Notes (And Where to Find Them)

*J*ohannes Gutenberg's invention of the European printing press in 1450 is considered by many to be the official end of the Dark Ages for Europe. Eventually, his invention would make it possible for ordinary people to own books, and along the way, sheet music also began being printed for ordinary musicians to own. Soon, people with a little musical know-how could teach themselves all the principles of music theory previously unavailable to those outside the institutions of religion or higher learning.

As the proficiency of the "common" musician increased, the need for more new sheet music increased as well. After composers learned they could turn a decent profit by selling multiple, machine-printed copies of their music — instead of one laboriously hand-drawn copy at a time — they began flooding the market with new compositions.

This evolution eventually led to the standardization of sheet music. For years, composers were free to use as many or as few staff lines as they wanted to express notation, but by the 1500s, the five-line staff that musicians use today was gradually becoming universally accepted, at least in Europe.

This chapter discusses the musical staves and where to find notes on them as well as the concept of half steps, whole steps, and accidentals. Mastering these concepts allows you to both navigate your way through a piece of sheet music and even begin to learn how to improvise.

Meeting the Staff, Clefs, and Notes

Notes and rests in music are written on what musicians call a *musical staff* (or staves, if you're talking about two). A staff is made of five parallel horizontal lines, containing four spaces between them, as shown in Figure 6-1.

© John Wiley & Sons, Inc.

Notes and rests are written on the lines and spaces of the staff. The particular musical notes that are meant by each line and space depend on which *clef* is written at the beginning of the staff. You may run across any of the following clefs (though the first two are the most common):

- ✔ Treble clef
- ✔ Bass clef
- ✔ C clefs, including alto and tenor

Think of each clef as a graph of *pitches,* or *tones,* shown as notes plotted over time on five lines and four spaces. Each pitch or tone is named after one of the first seven letters of the alphabet: A, B, C, D, E, F, G, A, B, C … and it keeps on going that way indefinitely, repeating the note names as the pitches repeat in *octaves.* The pitches ascend as you go from A to G, with every eighth note — where you return to your starting letter — signifying the beginning of a new octave.

The following sections give you more details on the clefs individually and together (called a grand staff). We also take a look at the C clef and when you might cross paths with it.

The treble clef

The *treble clef* is for higher-pitched notes. It contains the notes above middle C on the piano, which means all the notes you play with your right hand on the piano. On the guitar, the treble clef is usually the only clef you ever read. Most woodwind instruments, high brass instruments, and violins stick solely to the treble clef. Any instrument that makes *upper-register,* or high, sounds has its music written in the treble clef.

The treble clef is also sometimes called the *G clef.* Note that the shape of the treble clef itself resembles a stylized G. The loop on the treble clef also circles the second line on the staff, which is the note G, as shown in Figure 6-2.

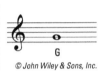

© John Wiley & Sons, Inc.

The notes are located in the treble clef on lines and spaces, in order of ascending pitch, as shown in Figure 6-3.

Figure 6-3:
The notes of the treble clef.

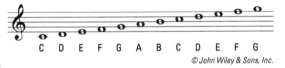

© John Wiley & Sons, Inc.

The bass clef

On the piano, the *bass clef* contains lower-pitched notes, the ones below middle C, including all the notes you play with your left hand on the piano. Music is generally written in the bass clef for lower wind instruments like the bassoon, the lower brass instruments like the tuba, and the lower stringed instruments like the bass guitar.

Another name for the bass clef is the *F clef.* The curly top of the clef partly encircles where the F note is on the staff, and it has two dots that surround the F note, as shown in Figure 6-4. (It also looks a bit like a cursive letter F, if you use your imagination.)

Figure 6-4:
The two dots of the bass clef surround the F note on the staff.

© John Wiley & Sons, Inc.

The notes on the bass clef are arranged in ascending order, as shown in Figure 6-5.

Figure 6-5:
The notes of the bass clef.

© John Wiley & Sons, Inc.

The grand staff and middle C

Put the treble and bass clefs together and you get the *grand staff,* as shown in Figure 6-6.

Figure 6-6:
The grand staff contains both the treble and bass clefs, connected by ledger lines and middle C.

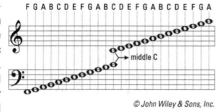

© John Wiley & Sons, Inc.

Middle C is located one line below the treble clef and one line above the bass clef. But it's not *in* either clef. Instead it's written on a ledger line. *Ledger lines* are lines written above the bass clef and below the treble clef that are necessary to connect the two clefs. Put it all together, and the notes flow smoothly from one clef to the other with no interruptions.

C clefs: Alto and tenor

Occasionally, you may come across an animal known as the *C clef.* The C clef is a moveable clef that you can place on any line of the staff. The line that runs through the center of the C clef, no matter which line that is, is considered middle C, as you can see in Figure 6-7.

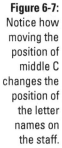

Figure 6-7: Notice how moving the position of middle C changes the position of the letter names on the staff.

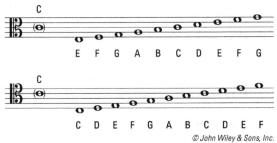

© John Wiley & Sons, Inc.

C clefs are preferred in classical notation for instrumental ranges that hover right above or right below middle C. Instead of having to constantly switch between reading treble and bass clefs, a musician has just one musical staff to read.

C clefs were more commonly used before sheet music was standardized and able to easily accommodate a wide range of tones. Today, the only C clefs commonly used are the following:

- ✔ **The alto clef:** Puts middle C on the third staff line; most commonly used for writing viola music.

- ✔ **The tenor clef:** Puts middle C on the next-to-the-top line of the staff; most commonly used for writing cello, trombone, and bassoon music.

Identifying Half Steps, Whole Steps, and Accidentals

In Western music, an octave is broken up into 12 tones called *half steps,* or *semitones.* But a musical *scale* contains seven notes, meaning that some of the distance between notes in a scale spans one semitone and some spans at least two semitones. In other words, some half steps are skipped when building scales. (Check out Chapter 7 for much more on scales.)

When musicians talk about the notes A, B, C, D, E, F, and G, they mean the *natural* notes — specifically, the notes that correspond to the white keys on a keyboard. The white keys of the keyboard were assigned the natural letter notes, which turn out to be the notes of the C major scale, beginning with C. However, because you're dealing with a musical vocabulary made up of 12 semitones, the keyboard also has five black keys, repeated over and over, which represent the semitones that are skipped in the C scale. The black keys were added much later than the original white keys in order to help build more perfect musical scales on the piano.

Moving a whole step on the piano or guitar means you move two half steps from your starting position. Half steps and whole steps are *intervals,* which we discuss in Chapter 9. Knowing the difference between whole steps and half steps is important when working with the patterns used to build scales and chords (covered in Chapters 7 and 10, respectively).

You also employ half steps when you come across an *accidental,* a notation used to raise or lower a natural note pitch. So when a note is *sharped,* you add a half step to the note; when a note is *flatted,* you remove a half step from the note.

Need a bit more info? We go into more detail about half steps, whole steps, and accidentals in the following sections.

Working with half steps

In Western musical notation, the smallest difference between two pitches is the *half step,* or semitone. Using the piano keyboard as a reference, if you pick a key, play it, and then play the key that's right next to it (on the left or right) whether that key is black or white, you've moved one half step in pitch. See Figure 6-8 for an illustration of this principle.

Strictly speaking, musical pitch is a continuous spectrum, because it's determined by the frequency of vibration (see Chapter 13). Therefore, many other *microtonal* sounds actually exist between consecutive half steps. Western musical notation recognizes only the division of pitch into half

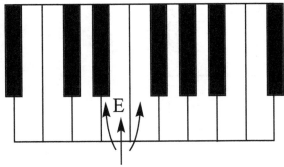

Figure 6-8:
Half steps are identified here to the left and right of the E key on the piano.

steps. In contrast, many Eastern instruments, particularly sitars and fretless stringed instruments, use *quarter tones.* Quarter tones are pitches located halfway between each half step.

As you can see in Figure 6-8, if you start out playing an E on the piano, a half step to the left brings you to E flat/D sharp. A half step to the right lands you on E sharp/F natural.

Half steps are even easier and more straightforward on the guitar: Each fret is a half step. You just move one fret up or one fret down from your starting point on any guitar string, and that move of one fret equals one half step. Moving down the neck (toward the headstock of the guitar) flats the note (Figure 6-9), while moving up the neck (toward the body) sharps it (Figure 6-10).

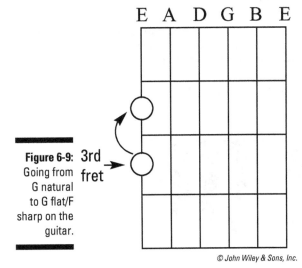

Figure 6-9:
Going from G natural to G flat/F sharp on the guitar.

3rd fret

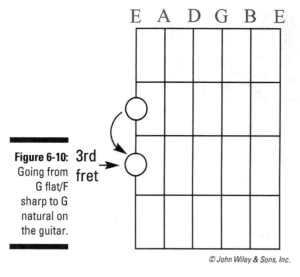

E A D G B E

Figure 6-10: Going from G flat/F sharp to G natural on the guitar.

3rd fret →

When a musician refers to a note being *flatted,* you know you need to move one half step to the left of that natural note; if it's being *sharped,* you know to move one half step to the right. Every black key on a piano has two names: It can be referred to as the flat of the white key on its right or the sharp of the white key on its left. It doesn't matter which way it's named. For example, while E flat and D sharp are written as different notes, they have the same pitch, or sound. Notes with the same pitch are referred to as *enharmonic.*

Taking whole steps

Following the logic that a half step on the piano or guitar is one key or fret away from the starting point (see the preceding section), it only makes sense that a whole step would be two keys or frets away from the starting point.

Say, for example, that you start on E on the keyboard. One whole step to the left of E would be D, as shown in Figure 6-11.

Figure 6-11: Moving one whole step, or two half steps, to the left of E on the piano brings you to D.

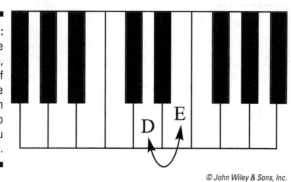

D E

Meanwhile, one whole step to the *right* of E would be F sharp, as shown in Figure 6-12.

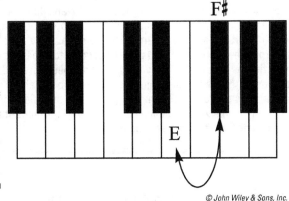

Figure 6-12: Moving one whole step, or two half steps, to the right of E on the piano brings you to F sharp.

On the guitar, a whole step is represented by a move of two frets up or down the neck.

The distance between the consecutive white piano keys E and F, and B and C, equal a half step, whereas the distance between the remaining white keys (G-A, A-B, C-D, D-E, F-G) is a whole step. That's because the piano is designed around the *C scale.*

Inventor Dr. Robert Moog's Thoughts on Keyboard Alternatives

"I think sound generation is a mature technology. Between analog and digital technology, you can make just about any sound you can imagine cheaply and easily. What we don't have cheap and easily yet are really good, new player interfaces — we're still working with the same old electronic organ principle. The same keyboards that were put into electronic organs 60 years ago are being used today, and there is very little difference. They feel the same, and, in fact, the organ keyboards that were developed in 1935 feel better than most keyboards that are designed today. A keyboard is just the starting point, especially if you think of all the ways that people like to move and push and touch when they're playing music. I think the field is wide open for developing really sophisticated, really human-oriented control devices.

(continued)

(continued)

But the problem for instrument designers is that people don't want to give up their keyboards. Millions of people know how to play the piano. It's what there is when you're learning how to play music. If somebody were to start off at the age of 30 or 40 or 50 and learn a new control device, they'd have to practice as much as they did when they were learning how to play the piano when they were kids. It's similar to the Dvorak keyboard, where you can type 20 or 30 percent faster than on a regular Qwerty keyboard. Anybody can do it, but very few people do it because it takes a certain amount of learning when you're an adult. Your mother's not going to teach you how to type on a Dvorak keyboard. Most adults already have plenty to do, and they're not going to relearn how to type. So new alternate controllers are like that, too. Designing them is going to be half the job — the other half is going to be musicians developing technique on those new interfaces. It's going to take decades."

Changing pitch with accidentals

Accidentals are notations used to raise or lower a natural note pitch on the staff by a half step. They apply to the note throughout a measure until you see another accidental. You can use these different types of accidentals:

- ✔ Sharps
- ✔ Flats
- ✔ Double sharps
- ✔ Double flats
- ✔ Naturals

For more specifics on these accidentals and what to do with them, keep reading.

Raising pitch with sharps

A *sharp* is shown in Figure 6-13.

Figure 6-13:
A sharp looks like a pound, or number, sign.

© John Wiley & Sons, Inc.

A sharp is placed before a note on the staff to indicate that the note is a half step higher, as shown in Figure 6-14.

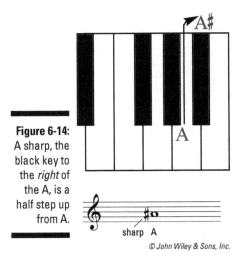

Figure 6-14:
A sharp, the black key to the *right* of the A, is a half step up from A.

© John Wiley & Sons, Inc.

Figure 6-15 shows a sharped E (the enharmonic of F natural). E sharp is one half step up in pitch from E.

Figure 6-15:
E to E sharp.

© John Wiley & Sons, Inc.

Using flats to lower pitch

You can see what a *flat* symbol looks like in Figure 6-16.

Figure 6-16:
A flat looks a bit like a lower-case *b*.

♭

© John Wiley & Sons, Inc.

A flat does just the opposite of a sharp: It lowers the note by a half step, as shown in Figure 6-17.

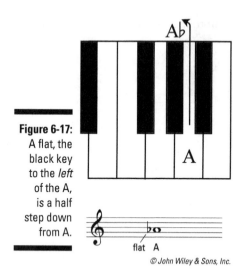

Figure 6-17:
A flat, the
black key
to the *left*
of the A,
is a half
step down
from A.

© John Wiley & Sons, Inc.

Figure 6-18 shows a flatted E. E flat is one half step down in pitch from E.

Figure 6-18:
E to E flat.

© John Wiley & Sons, Inc.

Doubling pitch with double sharps and flats

Every once in a while, you'll run into a *double sharp* or a *double flat,* which are shown in Figure 6-19.

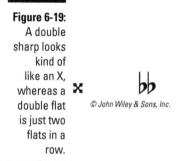

Figure 6-19:
A double
sharp looks
kind of
like an X,
whereas a
double flat
is just two
flats in a
row.

© John Wiley & Sons, Inc.

The notation on the left in Figure 6-19 is a double sharp, and the one on the right is a double flat. The double sharp raises the natural note two half steps — or one whole step — whereas the double flat lowers the note two half steps, or one whole step.

Cancelling sharps and flats with naturals

You may have heard of sharps and flats, but what is the natural (pictured in Figure 6-20)?

Figure 6-20:
A natural cancels out an already established sharp or flat.

© John Wiley & Sons, Inc.

When you see a natural sign next to a note, it means that any sharp or flat that's already in effect (either given in the key signature or in the same measure; see Chapter 8 for information on key signatures) is cancelled for the rest of the measure. In other words, you're supposed to play the "natural" version of the note instead of whatever sharp or flat was in effect, even if it was a double sharp or double flat.

Finding the Notes on the Piano and the Guitar

Sometimes you just can't remember which note is which when you're playing a musical instrument, especially when you're a beginner. But don't worry. You can use the figures in this section as a handy reference when you can't quite remember. We focus on the notes on the piano and the guitar because those instruments are the two most common that musicians pick up on their own when first learning to play music.

Looking for notes on the piano

Figure 6-21 shows a little more than three octaves' worth of the piano keyboard. The corresponding natural notes on the grand staff are labeled on the keyboard. (We discuss the grand staff in more detail earlier in this chapter.) Note also the hand placement, indicated above the keyboard (RH for right hand, and LH for left hand).

© John Wiley & Sons, Inc.

Figure 6-21:
The piano
keyboard,
matched
up with the
notes from
the grand
staff.

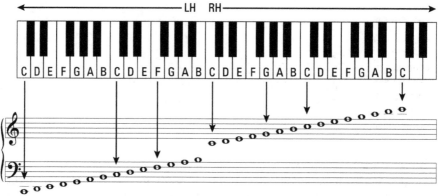

Picking out notes on the guitar

The trouble with laying out the neck of a guitar against musical notation is that notes repeat themselves all along the neck, and having so many options for playing notes in different ways can get confusing. So we've broken the guitar neck into three nonrepeating sections to correspond along the natural notes on the staff, stopping at the 12th fret (which usually has two dots on it). The 12th fret is also known as the *octave mark,* meaning it's the same note as the string played open, except one octave higher.

Figures 6-22 through 6-24 show the notes of the first three frets of the guitar, then the next five, and then the next four.

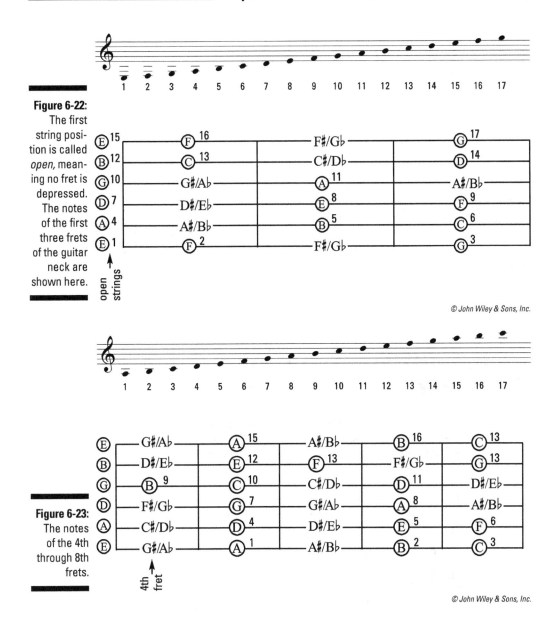

Figure 6-22:
The first string position is called *open,* meaning no fret is depressed. The notes of the first three frets of the guitar neck are shown here.

© John Wiley & Sons, Inc.

Figure 6-23:
The notes of the 4th through 8th frets.

© John Wiley & Sons, Inc.

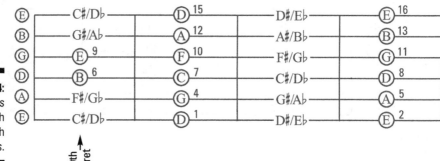

Figure 6-24: The notes of the 9th through 12th frets.

Using Mnemonics to Help Remember Notes

A zillion silly ways exist to remember the order of the notes along the musical staff. In fact, we probably have enough to build an entire book around. In this section, we provide just a few to get you going. Feel free to come up with your own *mnemonics* (memory helpers) to help keep things straight.

Here are some easy ways to remember the order of the notes of the treble clef staff lines, starting at the first line, on E, and heading up through G, B, D, and F on the top line of the staff:

- Every Good Boy Deserves Favor
- Every Good Boy Deserves Fudge
- Every Good Boy Does Fine
- Every Good Bird Does Fly

The notes in the spaces between the treble clef staff lines are easy to remember. They spell the word FACE, starting at the first space note, F, and heading up to the E in the top space on the staff. Everybody uses this one, and there's really no reason to try to come up with a complicated phrase when FACE is right there, staring you in the … well, you get it.

Here are some mnemonics for the notes on the bass clef staff lines, starting at the bottom note, G, and heading up to the A at the top:

- Go Buy Donuts For Al
- Good Boys Do Fine Always
- Great Big Dreams For America

For the space notes between the bass clef staff lines, just remember any one of the following:

- All Cows Eat Grass
- All Cars Eat Gas
- Alley Cats Eat Garbage

Chapter 7

Mastering the Major and Minor Scales

To put it simply, a *scale* is any group of consecutive notes that provides the material for part or all of a piece of music. We could write an entire encyclopedia on the different types of scales used in music from around the world, but because this book is primarily concerned with the Western tradition of music, we confine our discussion in this chapter to the two most frequently used scales: the major and the minor.

It's impossible to overemphasize just how important knowing your scales is to playing music. And it isn't enough to be able to play the scales back and forth and up and down, either. In order to successfully improvise or compose, you need to know how to jump around on your instrument and still land on all the right notes within the scale.

Say you're jamming with a group of musicians. If you know what key the rest of the band is playing in, and you know all the notes that are within that key (scales are determined by keys — you can read a lot more about keys and key signatures in Chapter 8), it's impossible to mess up so long as you stick to those notes. In fact, you can noodle all day in the proper key and sound like a regular Carlos Santana or Louis Armstrong.

Following Major-Scale Patterns

Even though every major scale contains a different set of notes, each scale is put together exactly the same way. The specific major-scale pattern of intervals is what makes them *major scales.*

Major scales follow the interval pattern of WWHWWWH, which means **Whole step Whole step Half step Whole step Whole step Whole step Half step.** We discuss half steps and whole steps at length in Chapter 6, but here's a quick refresher:

- ✔ **Half step:** Moving one piano key to the left or the right, or one guitar fret up or down.

- ✔ **Whole step:** Moving two piano keys to the left or the right, or two guitar frets up or down.

Pitchwise, a half-step is exactly $\frac{1}{12}$ of an octave, or 1 semitone. A whole step is exactly $\frac{1}{6}$ of an octave, or 2 semitones.

Each of the eight notes in a major scale is assigned a *scale degree* according to the order it appears in the scale:

- ✔ **1st note:** Tonic

- ✔ **2nd note:** Supertonic

- ✔ **3rd note:** Mediant

- ✔ **4th note:** Subdominant

- ✔ **5th note:** Dominant

- ✔ **6th note:** Submediant

- ✔ **7th note:** Leading tone (or leading note)

- ✔ **8th note:** Tonic

The 1st and 8th notes, the *tonics,* determine the name of the scale. (Scales that share the same starting notes are called *parallel scales.* For example, C major and C minor are parallel scales, because they both start on the same note: C.) Relative to the tonic note, the rest of the notes in the scale are usually attached to the numbers 2 through 7 (because 1 and 8 are already taken by the tonic). Each of these numbers represents a scale degree, and their pattern of whole steps and half steps determine the key of the scale.

The 1st and the 8th notes have the same name here because they're the exact same note — at the 8th note, the scale repeats itself. You won't hear a musician talk about the 8th degree of a scale — instead, she'll refer to the 1st note as the tonic.

So, for example, if you're playing a piece of music in the key of C major, which sequentially has the notes C, D, E, F, G, A, B, and C in it, and someone asks you to play the 4th and 2nd notes in the scales, you play an F and a D. And you do the same thing if that person asks you to play the subdominant and the supertonic.

Mastering scales is all about recognizing patterns on an instrument. If you look at a piano keyboard or the neck of a guitar, can you see where the 1, 2, 3, 4, 5, 6, 7, and 8 of each scale go? If you're given a scale and asked to play the sequence 5-3-2-1-6-4-5-8, do you know what notes you would play? Eventually, you want to be able to answer yes to these questions for all 12 major scales. Here's how:

- ✔ Picture each scale in your head and where it's located on your instrument.
- ✔ Know the letter name and number of each note in each scale.
- ✔ Be able to play sequences of notes when given the key and number.

Only when you can do all three things for the 12 major scales can you stop practicing your scales. In the following sections, we explain how to work with major scales on the piano and the guitar, and we point you toward audio tracks of the major scales.

The *major scale,* or the *diatonic scale,* is the most popular scale and the one that's the easiest to recognize when played. Songs like "Happy Birthday" and "Mary Had a Little Lamb" are composed in the major/diatonic scale.

Working with major scales on piano and guitar

If someone were to ask you to play the scale for C major on the piano, you would put it together like the one in Figure 7-1.

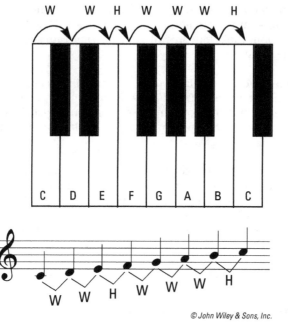

Figure 7-1: The C major scale, like all major scales, follows the WWHW-WWH pattern.

Notice the arrow pointing to the steps in the figure — every single major scale you work with follows this pattern, using different combinations of black and white keys on the piano, depending on the scale.

To play each major scale on the piano, begin with the piano key that is the name of the scale. For the A major scale, for example, you begin with the A. (If you haven't memorized the notes of the piano keyboard, refer to Chapter 6.) Then play the major scale pattern: WWHWWWH. The scale ends on the same note it began, only an octave higher.

To see the major scale for every key, refer to Chapter 8, which illustrates key signatures by showing the scale on the staff for each key. To hear all the major scales, listen to the audio tracks listed in the upcoming section "Listening to the major scales."

Playing scales on the guitar is even simpler than playing them on the piano. Guitarists think of the guitar neck as being broken up into blocks of four frets, and, depending on what key you want to play in, your hand is positioned over that block of four frets. Each four-fret block contains two octaves' worth of every pitch within that scale.

Major scales on the guitar follow the pattern shown in Figure 7-2, playing the notes in the number order they appear. ***Remember:*** The 8th note (tonic) of the first octave serves as the 1st note (tonic) of the second octave.

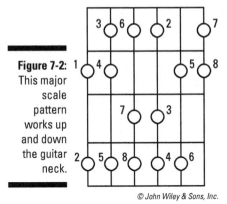

Figure 7-2:
This major scale pattern works up and down the guitar neck.

To play each scale on the guitar, begin with the correct fret on the first string (the top string as you hold the guitar, the low E string) to play the E major scale:

- **Open string:** E
- **1st fret:** F
- **2nd fret:** F♯/G♭
- **3rd fret:** G
- **4th fret:** G♯/A♭
- **5th fret:** A
- **6th fret:** A♯/B♭
- **7th fret:** B
- **8th fret:** C
- **9th fret:** C♯/D♭
- **10th fret:** D
- **11th fret:** D♯/E2♭
- **12th fret:** E
- **13th fret:** F

To play major scales on the guitar, you just move that pattern along the neck to build whatever major scale you'd like. You determine the key by the first and last notes of the scale, so if someone asks you to play a C major scale, you simply start the scale on the 8th fret. No black keys or white keys to fool with here — just the same pattern repeated along the neck, over and over. (To see the notes on the first 12 frets of a guitar, check out Chapter 6.)

The *actual* pitch of the guitar is one octave (12 half steps) lower than the *written* pitch. This discrepancy occurs simply because most sheet music is written for piano, so the notes would fall below the staff if they were accurately written for guitar. On the piano, the middle octave is the most frequently used and is therefore centered on the grand staff. If composers had to write guitar parts at their actual-sounding pitch, they would have to use too many ledger lines and the part would be confusing.

Listening to the major scales

Listen to Audio Tracks 1 through 15 to hear each of the major scales played on the piano and guitar. Note that F sharp and G flat, D flat and C sharp, and B and C flat are all enharmonic scales, or scales that sound the same as one another, but are notated differently, as in B and C flat major.

Audio Track	Scale
1	A major
2	A flat major
3	B major
4	B flat major
5	C major
6	C flat major
7	C sharp major
8	D major
9	D flat major
10	E major
11	E flat major
12	F major
13	F sharp major
14	G major
15	G flat major

Discovering All That Minor Scale Patterns Have to Offer

When you hear the term *minor scales,* you may be led to believe that this set of scales is much less important than the grand collection of major scales that we introduce earlier in this chapter. Or you may think the minor scales are only for sad, sappy songs. But the truth is that the arrangements and tones (or note sounds) available in the minor scales — divided, according to composition, into the natural, harmonic, and melodic minor scales — can be much more flexible for a composer to use than the major scales alone.

Even though every type of minor scale contains a different set of notes, each type of scale is put together in a specific way. These specific patterns of intervals are what put the minor scales into their little niche. The minor scale degrees all have the same names as the ones in major, except the 7th degree, which is called the *subtonic.*

Each of the eight notes in a minor scale has a name:

- ✔ **1st note:** Tonic
- ✔ **2nd note:** Supertonic
- ✔ **3rd note:** Mediant
- ✔ **4th note:** Subdominant
- ✔ **5th note:** Dominant
- ✔ **6th note:** Submediant
- ✔ **7th note:** Subtonic
- ✔ **8th note:** Tonic

In the harmonic and melodic minor scales, the 7th degree is called the *leading tone.* In the melodic minor scale, the 6th degree is called the *submediant.*

In the following sections, we discuss the natural, harmonic, and melodic minor scales and how to play them on the piano and the guitar.

Playing natural minor scales on piano and guitar

Natural minor scales follow the interval pattern of WHWWHWW, which translates into **W**hole step **H**alf step **W**hole step **W**hole step **H**alf step **W**hole step **W**hole step. The first note (and last) in the scale determines the scale name.

A natural minor scale is taken from the major scale of the same name, but with the 3rd, 6th, and 7th degrees lowered by one half step. So, for instance, if someone asks you to play the scale for A natural minor on the piano, you put it together as shown in Figure 7-3.

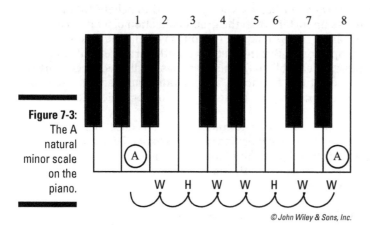

Figure 7-3: The A natural minor scale on the piano.

© John Wiley & Sons, Inc.

The same pattern also applies for each note up and down the guitar neck. Natural minor scales on the guitar follow the pattern shown in Figure 7-4. Play the notes in the number order shown in the figure. Your first note is indicated by the 1 shown on the first E string.

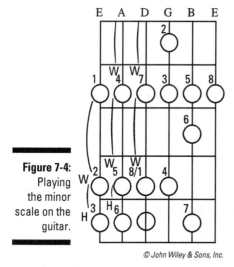

Figure 7-4: Playing the minor scale on the guitar.

© John Wiley & Sons, Inc.

Just as with major scales, to play natural minor scales on the guitar, you simply move the Figure 7-4 pattern along the neck of the guitar to build whatever minor scale you'd like. Whatever note you start with on the top (low E) string is the tonic and therefore names the scale. If someone asks you to play an A minor scale on the guitar, for example, you play the pattern shown in Figure 7-5.

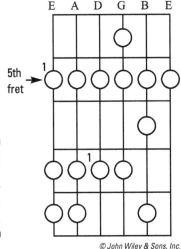

Figure 7-5: The A natural minor scale on the guitar.

© John Wiley & Sons, Inc.

Having fun with harmonic minor scales on piano and guitar

The *harmonic minor scale* is a variation of the natural minor scale (which we discuss in the preceding section). It occurs when the 7th note of the natural minor scale is raised by a half step. The step is *not* raised in the key signature; instead, it's raised through the use of accidentals (sharps, double sharps, or naturals). You can read about accidentals in Chapter 6.

To play the scale for A harmonic minor on the piano, you put the scale together as shown in Figure 7-6. Notice how the piano scale changes when you add a half step to the 7th scale degree.

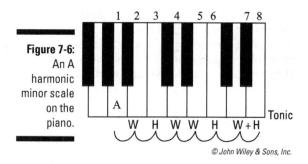

Figure 7-6:
An A
harmonic
minor scale
on the
piano.

© John Wiley & Sons, Inc.

When you're writing music and you want to use a harmonic scale, write it out using the natural minor key first (see preceding section), and then go back and add the accidental that raises the 7th degree up a half step.

Playing harmonic minor scales on the guitar is simple. You just position the pattern shown in Figure 7-7 over the root (tonic) position that you want to play in. Move it around to a different root to play the scale for that note.

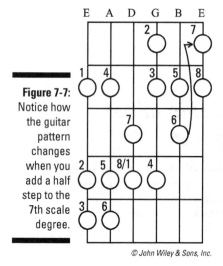

Figure 7-7:
Notice how
the guitar
pattern
changes
when you
add a half
step to the
7th scale
degree.

© John Wiley & Sons, Inc.

As always, the key is determined by the first and last notes of the scale, so if someone asks you to play an A harmonic minor scale on the guitar, you play what's shown in Figure 7-8.

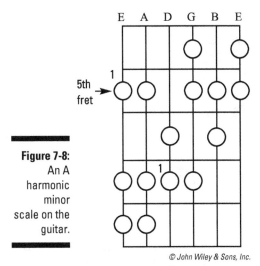

E   A   D   G   B   E

5th
fret →   1

1

Figure 7-8:
An A
harmonic
minor
scale on the
guitar.

© *John Wiley & Sons, Inc.*

Making great music with melodic minor scales on piano and guitar

The *melodic minor scale* is derived from the natural minor scale (see the earlier section "Playing natural minor scales on piano and guitar" for details). In the melodic minor scale, the 6th and 7th notes of the natural minor scale are each raised by one half step when going up the scale. However, keep in mind that they return to the natural minor when going down the scale.

This scale is a tricky one, so we're going to reiterate: While you're going up in pitch when playing a piece, you raise the 6th and 7th degrees of the natural minor scale a half step, but during parts of the same piece where the pitch goes down, you play the notes according to the natural minor scale. Scales in which the 6th and 7th degrees are flat in natural minor require naturals to raise those two degrees.

To play an A melodic minor scale ascending (going up) the piano, you play what's shown in Figure 7-9. Notice how the piano scale changes when you add a half step to both the 6th and 7th degrees.

When writing music in the melodic minor scale, composers write out the song using the natural minor pattern, and then they add the accidentals that modify any ascending 6th and 7th notes afterward.

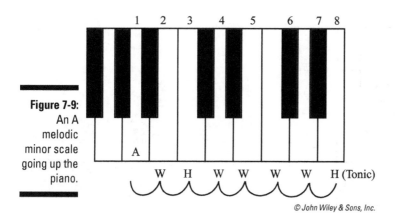

Figure 7-9:
An A melodic minor scale going up the piano.

© John Wiley & Sons, Inc.

The wonderful thing about the guitar is that you have to memorize only one pattern for each type of scale and you're set. To play the ascending A melodic minor scale on guitar, play the pattern as shown in Figure 7-10. To play an A melodic minor scale ascending on the guitar, you play it as shown in Figure 7-11.

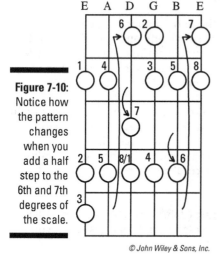

Figure 7-10:
Notice how the pattern changes when you add a half step to the 6th and 7th degrees of the scale.

© John Wiley & Sons, Inc.

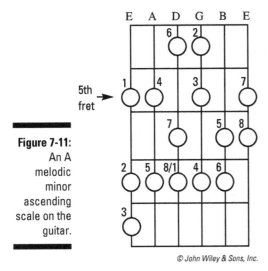

Figure 7-11:
An A melodic minor ascending scale on the guitar.

And, of course, for the descending notes on both the piano and guitar you revert to A natural minor.

Listening to the minor scales

Listen to Audio Tracks 16 through 60 to hear each of the minor scales played on piano and guitar.

Audio Track	Scale
16	A natural minor
17	A harmonic minor
18	A melodic minor
19	A flat natural minor
20	A flat harmonic minor
21	A flat melodic minor
22	A sharp natural minor
23	A sharp harmonic minor
24	A sharp melodic minor
25	B natural minor
26	B harmonic minor
27	B melodic minor

(continued)

(continued)

Audio Track	Scale
28	B flat natural minor
29	B flat harmonic minor
30	B flat melodic minor
31	C natural minor
32	C harmonic minor
33	C melodic minor
34	C sharp natural minor
35	C sharp harmonic minor
36	C sharp melodic minor
37	D natural minor
38	D harmonic minor
39	D melodic minor
40	D sharp natural minor
41	D sharp harmonic minor
42	D sharp melodic minor
43	E natural minor
44	E harmonic minor
45	E melodic minor
46	E flat natural minor
47	E flat harmonic minor
48	E flat melodic minor
49	F natural minor
50	F harmonic minor
51	F melodic minor
52	F sharp natural minor
53	F sharp harmonic minor
54	F sharp melodic minor
55	G natural minor
56	G harmonic minor
57	G melodic minor
58	G sharp natural minor
59	G sharp harmonic minor
60	G sharp melodic minor

Chapter 8

Key Signatures and the Circle of Fifths

*A*t the beginning of most pieces of written music, you find a group of sharps or flats located directly to the right of the time signature. This group of symbols is called the *key signature*, and it tells you in what key the song is written.

When you know a song's *key*, or the scale that the set of notes used to compose the song you're playing comes from, you may find reading the music easier. You can anticipate the notes on the sheet music based on your knowledge of the scales and the notes in those keys. Also, in a situation where you're playing with other musicians, if you know the key you're playing in and can anticipate the chords, you can guess where the melody of the song is going. It's almost like knowing what word is going to come next — or at least what limited selection of words could come next — to fit into a sentence.

In this chapter, you read about Pythagoras's Circle of Fifths and how to use it to read key signatures. You also find out all about key signatures and how to recognize them on sight. Finally, we round out the chapter with a discussion about major and minor key signatures and their relative minors and majors.

Understanding the Circle of Fifths and Recognizing Major Key Signatures

In the sixth century B.C., the Greek scholar and philosopher Pythagoras decided to try and make things easier for everyone by standardizing, or at least dissecting, musical tuning. He had already discovered the relationship between pitch frequencies and lengths of string and had defined what an octave was, so he figured standardizing tuning was the next logical step.

He divided a circle into 12 equal sections, like a clock. The result of his experimentation eventually became known as the Circle of Fifths, which is still used today. Each of the 12 points around the circle was assigned a pitch value, which roughly corresponds to the present system of an octave with 12 half steps. Western music theorists have since updated Pythagoras's Circle of Fifths to what you see in Figure 8-1.

Figure 8-1:
The Circle of Fifths shows the relationship between major keys and their relative minors.

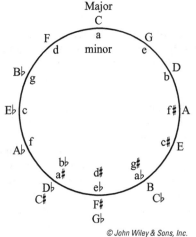

© John Wiley & Sons, Inc.

In mathematical terms, the unit of measure used in the circle is *cents*, with 1,200 cents equal to one octave. Each half step, then, is broken up into 100 cents.

The creation and use of the Circle of Fifths is the very foundation of modern Western music theory, which is why we talk about it so much in this book. Figure 8-2 shows a slightly different version of the Circle of Fifths than is shown in Figure 8-1. The former figure can be used to help you learn to read key signatures on sight by counting the sharps or flats in a time signature; you get the scoop on how to do so in the following sections.

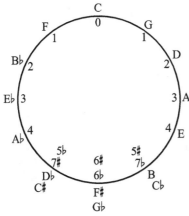

Figure 8-2:
The Circle of Fifths tells you how many sharps and flats are in the key signatures and scales of each key.

© John Wiley & Sons, Inc.

Each of the circle's 12 stops is actually the fifth pitch in the scale of the preceding stop, which is why it's called the Circle of Fifths. For example, the fifth pitch, or the *dominant* note, of the C scale is G. If you look at the Circle of Fifths in Figure 8-2, you can see that G is the next letter to the right of C. If you keep going clockwise, you see that the dominant note of the G scale, D, is the next stop, and so on around the circle. (You can find full coverage of scales in Chapter 7.)

Along with being your best friend for deciphering key signatures on sight, the Circle of Fifths is just as essential in writing music, because its clever design is helpful in composing and harmonizing melodies, building chords, and moving to different keys within a composition.

We can't emphasize enough how useful knowing the Circle of Fifths is. It's useful as a composer, as a performer, and as a student of music theory. All we can do is say it over and over and over: The Circle of Fifths — memorize it and use it.

The Circle of Fifths helps you figure out which sharps and flats occur in the different keys. The name of the key being played is the letter on the outside of the circle. In the following sections, be sure to notice that the order of sharps and flats given in the mnemonics are exactly the order in which they are written in key signatures.

Sharps: Father Charles Goes Down and Ends Battle

To figure out how many sharps are in each key, count *clockwise* from C at the top of the circle. C major has a number value of 0, so it has no sharps. G has a value of 1, so it has one sharp. When you play the G major scale on the piano, you play only white keys until you come to the seventh interval and land on that one sharp: F sharp, in this case. D has two sharps, A has three, and so on around the circle. The number value by each letter on the right-hand side of the circle represents how many sharps are in that key, which is determined by that key's scale. See Figure 8-3 to see the sharps going "up."

Figure 8-3:
The sharps are arranged in the key signature going "up."

© John Wiley & Sons, Inc.

The sharps always appear in a specific order in every key: F, C, G, D, A, E, B. You can easily remember this pattern of sharps by using the mnemonic *Father Charles Goes Down And Ends Battle.*

For example, if you're playing a song in the key of B major, you know from the Circle of Fifths that B major has five sharps. And you know from the *Father Charles* mnemonic that those sharps are F sharp, C sharp, G sharp, D sharp, and A sharp, because the sharps are always in that order. If you're playing the key of D major, which has two sharps, you know those sharps are F sharp and C sharp because *Father Charles.* . . . If you have a better mnemonic than the one we suggest, feel free to use it.

Flats: Battle Ends and Down Goes Charles's Father

For the major scales and keys with flats, you move counterclockwise around the Circle of Fifths, starting at C, which has a number value of 0. Therefore, the key of F major has one flat, the key of B flat major has two flats, and so on. Figure 8-4 shows the flats going "down."

Figure 8-4:
The flats are
arranged
in the key
signature
going
"down."

© *John Wiley & Sons, Inc.*

Like the sharps, the flats appear in a specific order in every key: B, E, A, D, G, C, F. The mnemonic we suggest here is *Battle Ends And Down Goes Charles's Father*, which is, as you likely notice, the exact reverse of the order of sharps in the circle (for more, see the preceding section on sharps). It's easy to remember that the first flat is always B flat because the flat sign itself looks kind of like a lowercase *b*, which is actually what it originally was.

So, G flat, for example, which is six steps away from C major on the circle, has six flats in its scale, and they are B flat, E flat, A flat, D flat, G flat, and C flat. The key of B flat, which is two steps away from C at the top of the circle, has B flat and E flat in its key.

Finding Minor Key Signatures and Relative Minors

The Circle of Fifths works the same way for *minor* keys as it does for major keys. The minor keys are represented by the lowercase letters *inside* the Circle of Fifths shown in Figure 8-1.

The minor keys on the inside of the circle are the *relative minors* of the major keys on the outside of the circle. The relative minor and its major key have the same key signature. The only difference is that the relative minor's scale starts on a different tonic, or first note. The *tonic*, or starting point, of a relative minor is a minor third — or three half steps — lower than its relative major key.

For example, C major's relative minor is A minor (refer to Figure 8-1, the Circle of Fifths where C is on the outside and A is on the inside of the circle). A minor's tonic note is A, which is three half steps to the left of C on the piano or three frets toward the head of the neck on the guitar.

Even the *Father Charles* and *Battle Ends* mnemonics that we describe earlier in this chapter stay the same when you're dealing with minor keys. No difference exists in the key signature between a major key and its relative minor.

On sheet music, the relative minor is the note one full line or space below the major key note. C is in the third space on the treble clef, and A, its relative minor, is in the second space, below it.

On the piano or guitar, a major chord and its relative minor go together like bread and butter. Many, many songs use this chord progression because it just sounds good. (You can find more about chords and chord progressions in Chapters 10 and 11.)

Visualizing the Key Signatures

Whether the key signatures are new to you or you're old chums, rehearsing never hurt anyone. In the following sections, we provide a rundown of the major and natural minor key signatures and a couple of octaves' worth of notes in those keys, arranged in a scale. Because this chapter focuses on the Circle of Fifths, we order the key signatures following the circle, as opposed to alphabetical order. We hope that going over these key signatures further cements them and the Circle of Fifths into your musical prowess.

Don't be thrown by the word *natural* when we use it to describe minor key signatures in this section. As we explain in Chapter 7, more than one kind of minor exists.

C major and A natural minor

Figure 8-5 shows the C major key signature, and Figure 8-6 shows the A natural minor key signature, C's relative natural minor.

Figure 8-5:
The C major key signature and scale.

© John Wiley & Sons, Inc.

Figure 8-6:
The A natural minor key signature and scale.

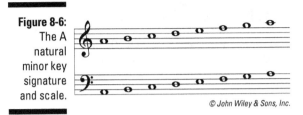

© John Wiley & Sons, Inc.

As you can see, the C major and the A natural minor have the same key signature (that is, no sharps and no flats) and the same notes in the scale because A is the relative natural minor of C. The only difference is that the C major scale starts on C, whereas the A natural minor scale starts on A.

G major and E natural minor

Figure 8-7 shows the G major key signature, and Figure 8-8 shows the E natural minor key signature, G's relative natural minor.

Figure 8-7:
The G major key signature and scale.

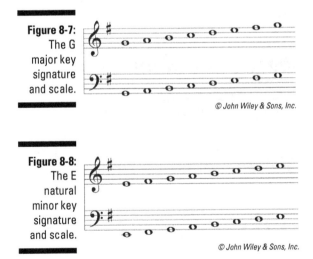

© John Wiley & Sons, Inc.

Figure 8-8:
The E natural minor key signature and scale.

© John Wiley & Sons, Inc.

You've now added one sharp (F) to the key signature. The next stop (D) has two (F and C, because *Father Charles . . .*), and you keep adding one more sharp until you get to the bottom of the Circle of Fifths.

D major and B natural minor

Figure 8-9 shows the D major key signature, and Figure 8-10 shows the B natural minor key signature, D's relative natural minor.

Figure 8-9:
The D major key signature and scale.

© John Wiley & Sons, Inc.

Figure 8-10:
The B natural minor key signature and scale.

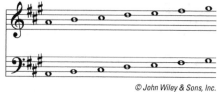

© John Wiley & Sons, Inc.

A major and F sharp natural minor

Figure 8-11 shows the A major key signature, and Figure 8-12 shows the F sharp natural minor key signature, A's relative natural minor.

Figure 8-11:
The A major key signature and scale.

© John Wiley & Sons, Inc.

Figure 8-12:
The F sharp natural minor key signature and scale.

© John Wiley & Sons, Inc.

E major and C sharp natural minor

Figure 8-13 shows the E major key signature, and Figure 8-14 shows the C sharp natural minor key signature, E's relative natural minor.

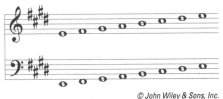

Figure 8-13:
The E major key signature and scale.

© John Wiley & Sons, Inc.

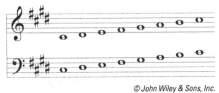

Figure 8-14:
The C sharp natural minor key signature and scale.

© John Wiley & Sons, Inc.

B/C flat major and G sharp/ A flat natural minor

Figure 8-15 shows the B major key signature and C flat major key signature. Figure 8-16 shows the G sharp natural minor key signature and the A flat natural minor key signature.

Figure 8-15:
The B major and C flat major key signatures and scales.

© John Wiley & Sons, Inc.

Figure 8-16:
The G sharp natural minor and A flat natural minor key signatures and scales.

Confused by the double naming here? Take a look at a keyboard, and you see that a black key doesn't exist for C flat. Instead, you see a white key: B. C flat and B are *enharmonic equivalents* of one another, meaning they're the same but with different names. All the notes in the key of B major and the key of C flat major sound exactly the same — they just use different musical notation. The same goes for G sharp natural minor and A flat natural minor — same notes, just different notation.

F sharp/G flat major and D sharp/ E flat natural minor

In the previous sections, you may have noticed that with each stop on the Circle of Fifths, one sharp is added to the key signature. From this point on, the number of flats in the key signature will be going down by one until returning to the 12 o'clock (C major/A natural minor) position.

Figure 8-17 shows the F sharp major key signature and the G flat major key signature. Figure 8-18 shows the D sharp natural minor key signature and the E flat natural minor key signature. More enharmonic equivalents (see preceding section)!

Figure 8-17:
The F sharp major and G flat major key signatures and scales.

Figure 8-18:
The D sharp natural minor and E flat natural minor key signatures and scales.

© John Wiley & Sons, Inc.

C sharp major/D flat and A sharp/ B flat natural minor

Figure 8-19 shows the C sharp major key signature and the D flat major key signature. Figure 8-20 shows the A sharp natural minor key signature and the B flat natural minor key signature.

Figure 8-19:
The C sharp major and D flat major key signatures and scales.

© John Wiley & Sons, Inc.

Figure 8-20:
The A sharp natural minor and B flat natural minor key signatures and scales.

© John Wiley & Sons, Inc.

These are the last of the enharmonic equivalent key signatures you have to remember. We promise. Also, these are the last of the keys with sharps in their signatures. In the remaining sections, you're working with flats alone as you continue going up the left side of the Circle of Fifths.

A flat major and F natural minor

Figure 8-21 shows the A flat major key signature and the F natural minor key signature, which is A flat's relative natural minor.

Figure 8-21:
The A flat major and F natural minor key signatures and scales.

E flat major and C natural minor

Figure 8-22 shows the E flat major key signature and the C natural minor key signature, which is E flat's relative natural minor.

Figure 8-22:
The E flat major and C natural minor key signatures and scales.

B flat major and G natural minor

Figure 8-23 shows the B flat major key signature and the G natural minor key signature, which is B flat's relative natural minor.

F major and D natural minor

Figure 8-24 shows the F major key signature and the D natural minor key signature, which is F major's relative natural minor.

Chapter 9

Intervals: The Distance Between Pitches

The distance between two musical pitches is called an *interval*. Even if you've never heard the word *interval* used in relation to music before, if you've listened to music, you've heard how intervals work with one another. If you've ever played music, or even just accidentally set a coffee cup down on a piano keyboard hard enough to make a couple of jangly notes sound out, you've worked with intervals. Scales and chords are both built from intervals. Music gets its richness from intervals. This chapter reviews the types of intervals most commonly used in music and discusses how intervals are used in building scales and chords.

Breaking Down Harmonic and Melodic Intervals

The following two types of intervals exist:

▶ A *harmonic interval* is what you get when you play two notes at the same time, as shown in Figure 9-1.

Figure 9-1:
A harmonic interval is two notes played simultaneously.

© John Wiley & Sons, Inc.

✔ A *melodic interval* is what you get when you play two notes separately in time, one after the other, as shown in Figure 9-2.

Figure 9-2:
A melodic interval is two notes played one after the other.

© John Wiley & Sons, Inc.

The *identity* of an interval, and this goes for both harmonic and melodic intervals, is determined by two things:

✔ Quantity

✔ Quality

We explain what we mean by each of these in the following sections.

Quantity: Counting lines and spaces

The first step in naming an interval is finding the distance between the notes as they're written on the staff. The *quantity,* or *number size,* of an interval is based on the number of lines and spaces contained by the interval on the music staff. Musicians and composers use different names to indicate the quantity of intervals:

✔ Unison (or prime)

✔ Second

- ✔ Third
- ✔ Fourth
- ✔ Fifth
- ✔ Sixth
- ✔ Seventh
- ✔ Octave

You determine an interval's quantity by simply adding up the lines and spaces included in the interval. You must count every line and every space between the notes as well as the lines or spaces that the notes are on. Accidentals don't matter when counting interval quantity.

Take a look at Figure 9-3 for an example of how easy it is to determine an interval's quantity. If you start on either the top or bottom note and count all the lines and spaces contained in the interval in the figure, including the lines or spaces that contain both notes, you end up with the number five. Therefore, the interval in Figure 9-3 has the quantity, or number size, of five, or a fifth. Because the notes are written together to be played at the same time, it's a *harmonic fifth*.

Figure 9-3:
The five lines and spaces in this interval's total quantity indicate this interval is a fifth.

© John Wiley & Sons, Inc.

Figure 9-4 shows a melodic second. Note that the sharp *accidental* (the ♯) on the F does absolutely nothing to the quantity of the interval. Interval quantity is only a matter of counting the lines and spaces. (You can read about accidentals in Chapter 6.)

Figure 9-4:
The fact that
the first note
is F sharp
doesn't
affect the
quantity of
the interval.

© John Wiley & Sons, Inc.

Figure 9-5 shows interval quantities from unison (the two notes are the same) to octave (the two notes are exactly an octave apart) and all the intervals in between. Sharps and flats are thrown in for fun, but remember, they don't matter when it comes to interval quantity.

Figure 9-5:
Melodic
intervals in
order from
left to right:
unison,
second,
third, fourth,
fifth, sixth,
seventh,
and octave.

© John Wiley & Sons, Inc.

What if an interval spans more than one octave? In that case, it's called a *compound interval.* As with all interval quantities, you just count the lines and spaces for a compound interval. The example shown in Figure 9-6 has the quantity of ten and is therefore called a *tenth.* (We discuss compound intervals in more detail later in this chapter.)

Figure 9-6:
A compound
interval with
a total quan-
tity of ten
and is called
a tenth.

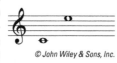

© John Wiley & Sons, Inc.

Quality: Considering half steps

Interval *quality* is based on the number of half steps from one note to another. Unlike in interval quantity (see the previous section), accidentals (sharps and flats), which raise or lower a pitch by a half step, do matter in interval quality. (See Chapter 6 for details on half steps and accidentals.) Interval quality gives an interval its distinct sound.

Each of the intervals shown in Figure 9-7 has exactly the same quantity, but they sound different because each one has a different quality.

Figure 9-7:
All these
intervals are
fifths, but
the various
qualities of
the fifths
make them
sound
different.

© John Wiley & Sons, Inc.

Play Audio Track 61 to hear the differences between the intervals that have the same quantity (fifth) but different qualities.

The terms used to describe quality, and their abbreviations, are as follows:

- ✔ **Major (M):** Contains two half steps between notes

- ✔ **Minor (m):** Contains a half step less than a major interval, or one half step between notes

- ✔ **Perfect (P):** Refers to the harmonic quality of unisons, octaves, fourths, and fifths (which we describe later in this chapter)

- ✔ **Diminished (dim or d):** Contains a half step less than a minor or perfect interval

- ✔ **Augmented (aug or A):** Contains a half step more than a major or perfect interval

Naming intervals

Every interval gets its full name from the combination of both the quantity and the quality of the interval. For example, you may encounter a *major third* or a *perfect fifth*. Here are the possible combinations that you use when describing intervals:

- ✔ Perfect (P) can only be used with unisons, fourths, fifths, and octaves.

- ✔ Major (M) and minor (m) can only be used with seconds, thirds, sixths, and sevenths (which we discuss later in this chapter).

- ✔ Diminished (dim) can be used with any interval, with the exception of unisons.

- ✔ Augmented (aug) can be used with any interval.

Looking at Unisons, Octaves, Fourths, and Fifths

Unisons, octaves, fourths, and fifths share the same characteristics in that they all use the terms perfect, augmented, or diminished to identify their quality. (See the earlier section "Quality: Considering half steps" for more information.)

Perfect unisons

A *perfect melodic unison* is possibly the easiest move you can make on an instrument (except for a rest, of course). You just press a key, pluck, or blow the same note twice. You can play unisons on most stringed instruments because the same note occurs more than once on these instruments, such as on the guitar (the fifth fret on the low E string is the same as the open A string, for example).

In music written for multiple instruments, a *perfect harmonic unison* occurs when two (or more) people play exactly the same note, in the exact same manner, on two different instruments.

Augmented unisons

To make a perfect unison augmented, you add one half step between the notes. You can alter either of the notes in the pair to increase the distance between the notes by a half step.

The interval from B flat to B is called an *augmented unison* (or *augmented prime*) — *unison* because the note names are the same (both Bs) and *augmented* because the interval is one half step greater than a perfect unison.

A diminished unison doesn't exist, because no matter how you change the unisons with accidentals, you're still adding half steps to the total interval.

Octaves

When you have two notes with an interval quantity of eight lines and spaces, you have an *octave*. A *perfect octave* is a lot like a perfect unison (see the earlier section "Perfect unisons") in that the same note (on a piano, it would be the same white or black key on the keyboard) is being played. The only difference is that the two notes are separated by 12 half steps, including the starting note, either above or below the starting point.

The perfect melodic octave in Figure 9-8 has 12 half steps between the notes.

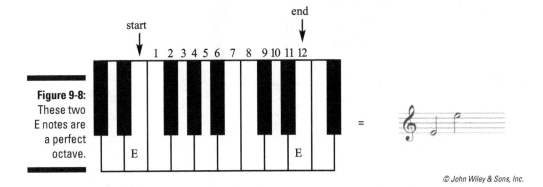

Figure 9-8: These two E notes are a perfect octave.

© John Wiley & Sons, Inc.

To make a perfect octave augmented, you increase the distance between the notes by one more half step. Figure 9-9 shows an augmented octave from E to E sharp. It was augmented by raising the top note a half step so that 13 half steps come between the first note and the last. You could also make an augmented octave by lowering the bottom E note a half step to E flat.

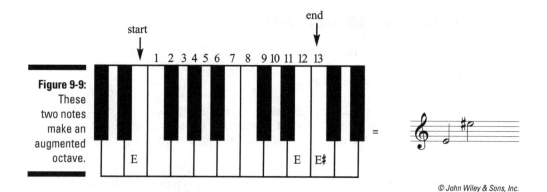

Figure 9-9: These two notes make an augmented octave.

© John Wiley & Sons, Inc.

To make the same octave diminished, you *decrease* the distance between the notes by one half step. For example, Figure 9-10 illustrates lowering the top note a half step so that only 11 half steps come between the first note and the last. You could also raise the bottom note by a half step to make another diminished octave.

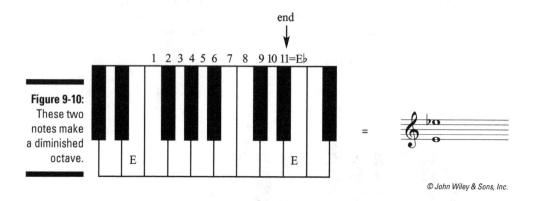

Figure 9-10: These two notes make a diminished octave.

© John Wiley & Sons, Inc.

Fourths

Fourths are pairs of notes separated by four lines and spaces. All fourths are perfect in quality, containing five half steps between notes — except for the fourth from F natural to B natural, which contains *six* half steps (making it an *augmented fourth*). Compare the note pairs in Figure 9-11 on the keyboard to see what we mean.

Figure 9-11:
Fourths as
seen on the
staff with
the special
(augmented)
case of the
F natural
and the
B natural
circled.

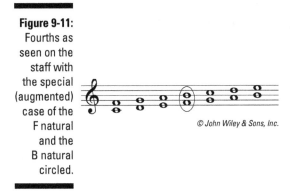

© John Wiley & Sons, Inc.

Figure 9-12 shows the connection between each fourth on a keyboard. Note that unlike the rest, the F natural and B natural require six half steps.

Figure 9-12:
On the
keyboard,
every
natural
fourth is
a perfect
fourth
(except for
the interval
between F
natural and
B natural).

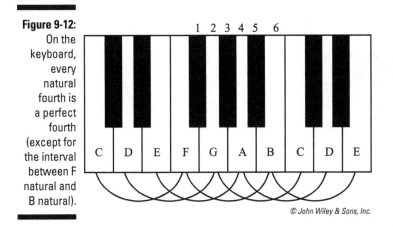

© John Wiley & Sons, Inc.

Because augmented fourths are a half step larger than perfect fourths, you can create a perfect fourth between the notes F natural and B natural by either raising the bottom note to F sharp or lowering the top note to B flat.

If the natural fourth is perfect, adding the same accidental (either a sharp or a flat) to both notes doesn't change the interval's quality. It stays a perfect fourth. The same number of half steps (five) occurs between D natural and

G natural that occurs between D sharp and G sharp, or D flat and G flat, as shown in Figures 9-13 and 9-14. If one note changes but the other doesn't, the quality of the interval does change.

Figure 9-13: Adding accidentals to both notes in a perfect fourth interval doesn't change it from being a perfect fourth.

Figure 9-14: You can see on a keyboard the same principle shown in Figure 9-13.

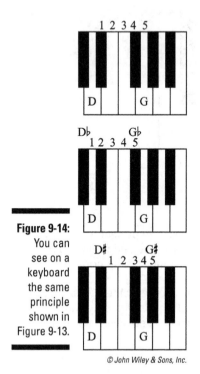

Fifths

Fifths are pairs of notes separated by five lines and spaces (as shown in Figure 9-15). Fifths are pretty easy to recognize in notation, because they're two notes that are exactly two lines or two spaces apart.

Figure 9-15:
Fifths have an interval quantity of five lines and spaces.

© John Wiley & Sons, Inc.

All fifths are *perfect* fifths, meaning that the interval contains seven half steps. However, as you may have guessed, the interval between B to F is a *diminished fifth,* which turns out to have the same sound as an augmented fourth. Only six half steps occur between those two notes whether you're going from F natural to B natural or B natural to F natural.

You can create a perfect fifth between F natural and B natural by adding one more half step — either by turning the B natural to a B flat or by raising the F natural to an F sharp. This time, because the notes are flipped around from the order they appeared in the interval of fourths, both changes *increase* the size of the interval.

Again, just as in a perfect fourth, if a fifth is perfect (every case except F natural and B natural), adding the same accidentals to both notes in the interval doesn't change its quality. And, as with fourths, if only one of the notes is altered with an accidental, the quality does change.

Recognizing Seconds, Thirds, Sixths, and Sevenths

Seconds, thirds, sixths, and *sevenths* all share the characteristic of using the terms *major, minor, augmented,* and *diminished* to identify their quality. (Check out the earlier section "Quality: Considering half steps" for more information.)

A major interval made *smaller* by one half step becomes minor, whereas a major interval made *larger* by one half step becomes augmented. A minor interval made *larger* by one half step becomes major, and a minor interval made *smaller* by one half step becomes diminished.

Clear as mud, right? Well, don't worry. We tell you everything you need to know in the following sections. Also, Table 9-1 summarizes the intervals from unison to octave. Notice in the table that the identity of the interval itself depends on the quantity of the interval number — that is, how many lines and spaces are included in the total interval.

Table 9-1	Intervals from Unison to Octave
Half Steps between Notes	*Interval Name*
0	Perfect unison/diminished second
1	Augmented unison/minor second
2	Major second/diminished third
3	Augmented second/minor third
4	Major third/diminished fourth
5	Perfect fourth/augmented third
6	Augmented fourth/diminished fifth
7	Perfect fifth/diminished sixth
8	Augmented fifth/minor sixth
9	Major sixth/diminished seventh
10	Augmented sixth/minor seventh
11	Major seventh/diminished octave
12	Augmented seventh/perfect octave
13	Augmented octave

Seconds

When you have two notes with an interval quantity of two lines and spaces, you have a *second*, as you can see in Figure 9-16. Seconds are pretty easy to recognize — they're the two notes perched right next to each other, one on a line and one in a space.

Figure 9-16:
These three
sets of
notes are all
seconds.

© John Wiley & Sons, Inc.

If one half step (one piano key or one guitar fret) exists between seconds, the interval is a *minor second* (m2). If two half steps (one whole step, or two adjacent piano keys or guitar frets) exist between seconds, the interval is a *major second* (M2).

For example, the interval between E natural and F natural is a minor second, because one half step occurs between those two notes (see Figure 9-17).

Figure 9-17:
The interval
between
E and F is
a minor
second,
because it
only con-
tains one
half step.

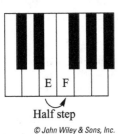

© John Wiley & Sons, Inc.

Meanwhile, the interval between F and G is a major second, because two half steps (one whole step) exist between those two notes, as illustrated in Figure 9-18.

Figure 9-18:
The interval
between
F and G
is a major
second,
because
it contains
two half
steps.

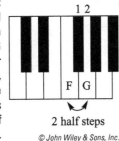

© John Wiley & Sons, Inc.

A major second is made minor by decreasing its quantity by one half step. You can decrease its quantity either by lowering the top note a half step or raising the bottom note a half step. Both moves reduce the distance between the notes to one half step (one piano key or one guitar fret), as Figure 9-19 shows.

Figure 9-19:
Turning a major second into a minor second.

© John Wiley & Sons, Inc.

A minor second can be turned into a major second by increasing the interval size by one half step. You can increase the interval size either by raising the top note a half step or by lowering the bottom note a half step. Both moves make the distance between the notes two half steps (two piano keys or three guitar frets).

The only place that half steps occur between white-key seconds is from E natural to F natural and B natural to C natural — the two spots on the keyboard where there are no black keys between the two white keys.

Adding the same accidental to both notes of a natural second doesn't change its quality. All the seconds shown in Figure 9-20 are major seconds.

Figure 9-20:
Major seconds.

© John Wiley & Sons, Inc.

All the seconds shown in Figure 9-21 are minor seconds.

Figure 9-21:
Minor seconds.

© John Wiley & Sons, Inc.

An augmented second (A2) is one half step larger than a major second. In other words, three half steps exist between each note. You turn a major second into an augmented second either by raising the top note or lowering the bottom note one half step, as shown in Figures 9-22 and 9-23.

Figure 9-22:
Turning a major second interval into an augmented second.

© John Wiley & Sons, Inc.

Figure 9-23:
Turning a major second interval into an augmented second on the piano: F to G sharp, and F flat to G.

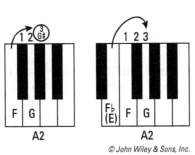

© John Wiley & Sons, Inc.

A diminished second is one half step smaller than a minor second — meaning no steps occur between each note. They're the same note. A diminished second is an enharmonic equivalent of a perfect unison. An *enharmonic* means that you're playing the same two notes, but the notation for the pair is different.

Thirds

Thirds occur when you have an interval that contains three lines and spaces as Figure 9-24 does.

Figure 9-24:
Thirds are
located on
adjacent
lines or
spaces.

© John Wiley & Sons, Inc.

If a third contains four half steps, it's called a *major third* (M3). Major thirds occur from C to E, F to A, and G to B. If a third contains three half steps, it's called a *minor third* (m3). Minor thirds occur from D to F, E to G, A to C, and B to D. Figure 9-25 shows major and minor thirds on the musical staff.

Figure 9-25:
Major and
minor thirds
on the staff.

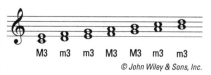

© John Wiley & Sons, Inc.

A major third can be turned into a minor third if you decrease its interval size by one half step, making the total three half steps between notes. You can decrease its interval size either by lowering the top note a half step or raising the bottom note a half step (see Figure 9-26).

Figure 9-26:
Turning a
major third
into a minor
third.

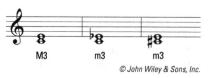

© John Wiley & Sons, Inc.

A minor third can be turned into a major third by adding one more half step to the interval, either by — you guessed it — raising the top note a half step or by lowering the bottom note a half step, as shown in Figure 9-27.

Figure 9-27:
Turning a minor third into a major third.

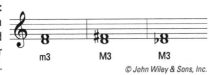

© John Wiley & Sons, Inc.

As with seconds, fourths, and fifths, the same accidental added to both notes of a third (both major and minor) doesn't change its quality; adding an accidental to just one of the notes of a third does change its quality.

An augmented third (A3) is a half step larger than a major third, with five half steps between notes. Starting from a major third, raise the upper note a half step or lower the bottom note a half step. Figure 9-28 shows augmented thirds. An augmented third is also the enharmonic equivalent of a perfect fourth — they're the same note, but the notation is different.

Figure 9-28:
Turning a major third into an augmented third.

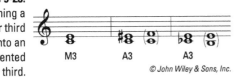

© John Wiley & Sons, Inc.

A diminished third is a half step smaller than a minor third. Beginning with a minor third, either raise the bottom note a half step or lower the upper note a half step, making for an interval of two half steps (see Figure 9-29).

Figure 9-29:
Turning a minor third into a diminished third.

© John Wiley & Sons, Inc.

Sixths and sevenths

When you have two notes with an interval quantity of six lines and spaces, as in Figure 9-30, you have a *sixth*. The notes in a sixth are always separated by either two lines and a space or two spaces and a line.

© John Wiley & Sons, Inc.

When you have two notes with an interval quantity of seven lines and spaces, as in Figure 9-31, you have a *seventh*. Sevenths always consist of a pair of notes that are both on lines or spaces. They're separated by either three lines or three spaces.

© John Wiley & Sons, Inc.

Building Intervals

The first step in building any interval when creating a piece of music is to create the desired quantity, or number size, above or below a given note. Then you determine the quality. We detail each of these steps in the following sections.

Determining quantity

Determining quantity is easy, especially on paper. For, say, a unison interval, just pick a note. Then, right next to the first note, put another one exactly like it.

Want to make your interval an octave? Put the second note exactly seven lines and spaces above or below the first, making for a total interval quantity of eight lines and spaces, as shown in Figure 9-32.

Figure 9-32:
Octaves of the note G (spanning the two clefs, with middle C indicated).

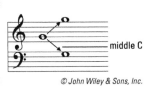

middle C

© John Wiley & Sons, Inc.

How about a fourth? Put the second note three spaces and lines above or below the first note, making for a total interval quantity of four lines and spaces. And a fifth? Put the second note four spaces and lines above or below the first note, making for a total interval quantity of five lines and spaces.

Establishing the quality

The second step to building an interval is to decide what the quality of the interval will be. Say, for example, your starting note is an A flat. And suppose you want your interval to be a perfect fifth above A flat. First, you count out the *quantity* needed for the fifth interval, meaning you count an additional four spaces above the starting note, making for a total quantity of five lines and spaces, as shown in Figure 9-33.

Figure 9-33:
Figuring out the quantity needed to build a perfect fifth above A flat.

= fifth

© John Wiley & Sons, Inc.

Next, you have to alter the second note in order to make it a perfect fifth. Because all fifths are perfect so long as both notes have the same accidental (except for darned B and F), in order to make this pair a perfect fifth, you have to flat the second note so it matches the first, as shown in Figure 9-34.

Figure 9-34:
Flatting the
second note
to match the
first makes
a perfect
fifth.

© John Wiley & Sons, Inc.

If you want to make the second note an augmented fifth (abbreviated aug5 or A5) *below* A, you count *down* an additional four lines and spaces from A to make a total quality of five lines and spaces, and then you write the note, which is D. See Figure 9-35.

Figure 9-35:
Building an
augmented
fifth below
A starts with
finding the
quantity.

© John Wiley & Sons, Inc.

Now you alter your added note to make the interval augmented. As you now know, a fifth is an augmented fifth when an additional half step is added to the interval ($7 + 1 = 8$ half steps), so you would lower the bottom note to a D flat, as shown in Figure 9-36.

Figure 9-36:
Adding the
accidental
makes the
interval
augmented.

© John Wiley & Sons, Inc.

To make the second note a diminished fifth (abbreviated dim5 or D5) *above* A, you count *up* an additional four lines and spaces, to make a total quality of five lines and spaces, and then write the note, which is E.

Finally, you alter your added note to make the interval diminished. A fifth is a diminished fifth when a half step is removed from the perfect fifth ($7 - 1 = 6$ half steps), so you would lower the top note to an E flat, as shown in Figure 9-37. (Note that a diminished fifth is the same as an augmented fourth — both intervals are made up of six half steps.)

Figure 9-37:
Adding the accidental makes the fifth diminished.

© John Wiley & Sons, Inc.

Showing Major and Perfect Intervals in the C Major Scale

A *scale* is really nothing more than a specific succession of intervals, starting from the first note of the scale, or the *tonic* note. Getting comfortable with intervals and their qualities is the first step to mastering scales and chords. (See Chapter 7 for much more on major and minor scales.)

Table 9-2, using the C major scale as an example, illustrates the relationship between the first note and every interval used in a major scale.

Table 9-2	**Intervals in the C Major Scale**	
Note	*Interval from Tonic*	*Note Name*
First note (tonic)	Perfect unison	C
Second note	Major 2nd (M2)	D
Third note	Major 3rd (M3)	E
Fourth note	Perfect 4th (P4)	F
Fifth note	Perfect 5th (P5)	G
Sixth note	Major 6th (M6)	A
Seventh note	Major 7th (M7)	B
Eighth note	Perfect octave (P8)	C

Figure 9-38 shows the intervals from Table 9-2 on the musical scale. These intervals are found in the same order in any major scale. In the major scale, only major and perfect intervals occur above the tonic note. Knowing this can make identifying the qualities of intervals much easier. If the top note of an interval is in the major scale of the bottom note, it must be major (if it's a second, third, sixth, or seventh) or perfect (if it's a unison, fourth, fifth, or octave).

Figure 9-38:
Simple
intervals in
the C major
scale.

M2   M3   P4   P5   M6   M7   P8

© John Wiley & Sons, Inc.

Listen to Audio Track 62 to hear simple intervals in the C major scale.

Checking Out Compound Intervals

The phrase *compound interval* can sound a bit complicated and scary — maybe because of the word *compound* itself. Yet, the truth of the matter is that creating compound intervals won't be completely foreign if you're familiar with any other interval we discuss in this chapter.

What distinguishes a *compound interval* from other intervals is that a compound interval is not confined to one octave the way a simple interval is. A compound interval can be spread out over several octaves, although the notes of the chords most often just come from two neighboring octaves. The following sections outline just how to build a compound interval and return it to a simple state.

Creating a compound interval

Just how do you go about building a compound interval? You have two options:

- Count the interval between notes by half steps, as with the tenth in Figure 9-6.

- Take your compound interval, put both notes in the same octave, figure out the number size of that interval, and then add seven to the number size of the resulting interval.

Here's an example of how to create a compound interval using this second method: Take a look at the simple intervals in the C major scale in Figure 9-38. Now, turn each of those figures into a compound interval by adding an octave to the second note in each example. When we add an octave to a major second interval (M2), it becomes a major ninth (M9). When we add an octave to a major third (M3), it becomes a major tenth (M10). A perfect fourth (P4) becomes a perfect eleventh (P11), while a perfect fifth (P5) becomes a perfect twelfth (P12). The quality of the interval remains the same — all that's been done is an extra octave's been added to the quantity (+7). (See Figure 9-39.)

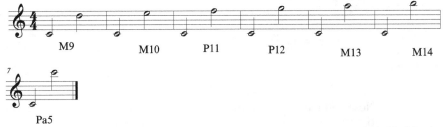

Figure 9-39: Major compound intervals in the C major scale.

M9 M10 P11 P12 M13 M14

Pa5

The first note in the simple intervals in Figure 9-38 is exactly the same as the first note in the compound intervals in Figure 9-39. The second note in the compound interval is the same note as the second note in the simple interval in Figure 9-38, just one octave higher. The quality of each interval remains the same, but the size number has increased by one octave, or the original number plus 7.

If you were to increase the distance between the notes by yet another full octave, you would simply add 7 to the size number again to reflect the interval size: Major 16, Major 17, Perfect 18, Perfect 19, Major 20, Major 21, and Perfect 22.

Returning a compound to its simple state

Finding the quantity and quality of a compound interval is very similar to the process you can use to build a compound interval (see the preceding section). Just reduce the compound interval to a simple interval by putting both notes in the same octave, either by moving the first note up or the second note down.

Here's how it works: In Figure 9-40, you have a compound interval of unknown quantity and quality. If you don't mind counting out all the lines and spaces (10) between the two notes (C and E sharp) to find the quantity, then you don't have to reduce the interval to a simple interval. However, most people find it easier to figure out the quantity and quality of an interval if the notes are closer together on the staff.

Figure 9-40:
The original compound interval of unknown quantity and quality.

© John Wiley & Sons, Inc.

Now, reduce the compound interval to a simple interval by simply bringing the two notes closer together so that they're in the same octave. You can either bring the first note up an octave, as shown in Figure 9-41, or the second note down an octave, as shown in Figure 9-42.

Figure 9-41:
Reducing the compound interval into a simple interval.

© John Wiley & Sons, Inc.

Figure 9-42:
Another way to reduce the compound interval into a simple interval.

© John Wiley & Sons, Inc.

In its reduced state, the quantity of the interval pictured in Figure 9-42 is a third. When you take a third and raise the upper note a half step or lower the bottom note a half step, the interval becomes an augmented third (A3). Add an octave, and the compound interval's quantity and quality is an A10, or the simple interval quantity and quality, plus 7. Quality has no bearing on octave displacement — only the quantity changes.

Chapter 10

Chord Building

A chord is, quite simply, three or more notes played together or, in the case of arpeggiated chords, one after another. By this simple definition, banging a coffee cup or your elbow on top of three or more piano keys at the same time makes a chord — it probably doesn't sound particularly musical, but it's still technically a chord.

To the uninitiated and experienced performer alike, chord construction can sometimes seem like magic. There's something absolutely beautiful and amazing about the way the individual notes in a chord work to enhance one another. Most people don't appreciate a properly played chord until they hear the way "wrong" notes sound against each other — for example, your coffee cup pushing onto the piano keyboard in a poorly constructed chord.

In most Western music, chords are constructed from *consecutive intervals of a third* — that is, each note in a chord is a third apart from the one before and/or after it (see Chapter 9 if you need a refresher on your intervals). Figure 10-1 illustrates two stacks of thirds to show you what we mean.

Figure 10-1:
Two stacks
of thirds,
one on the
lines and
the other in
the spaces.

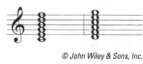

© John Wiley & Sons, Inc.

With chords based on intervals of a third, all the notes are either going to be line notes or space notes, resting one on top of another like the examples in Figure 10-1.

Creating Triads with Three Pitches

Triads, which consist of any three pitches from the same scale, are the most common type of chord used in music. Here are the different types of triads you'll likely work with:

- ✔ Major
- ✔ Minor
- ✔ Augmented
- ✔ Diminished

In the following sections, we provide information on these triads, but first we introduce what triads are and what they're made of.

Roots, thirds, and fifths

The term *triad* refers to chords that contain three different pitches and are built of thirds. The bottom note of a triad is called the *root;* many beginning music students are taught to think of a triad as being a tree, with the root of a triad being its, well, root. Chords carry the letter name of the root note, as in the root of a *C chord,* shown in Figure 10-2.

Figure 10-2:
The root of
a C chord
(either C
could be the
root).

© John Wiley & Sons, Inc.

Play Track 63 to hear the root of a C chord.

The second note of a triad is the *third* (see Chapter 9 for more information about intervals). The third of a chord is referred to as such because it's a third interval away from the root of the chord. Figure 10-3 shows the root and major third of a C chord.

Figure 10-3:
The root and
major third
of a C major
chord.

© John Wiley & Sons, Inc.

Play Track 64 to hear the root and major third of a C chord.

The third of a chord is especially important in constructing chords, because it's the *quality* of the third that determines whether you're dealing with a major or minor chord. (We discuss quality more in Chapter 9.)

The last note of a triad is the *fifth*. This note is referred to as a fifth because it's a fifth from the root, as shown in Figure 10-4.

Figure 10-4:
The root and
fifth of a C
major chord.

© John Wiley & Sons, Inc.

Play Track 65 to hear the root and fifth of a C major chord.

Combine the root, third, and fifth, and you have a triad, such as those shown in Figure 10-5.

Figure 10-5:
C major
triads.

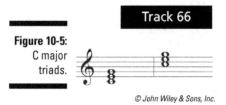

© John Wiley & Sons, Inc.

Play Track 66 to hear a C major triad.

The following sections walk you through building a variety of different triads: major, minor, augmented, and diminished. Table 10-1 has a handy chart to help you keep the formulas straight.

Table 10-1	Building Triads
Building Triads by Counting Half Steps	
Major =	Root position + 4 half steps + 3 half steps (7 half steps above root)
Minor =	Root position + 3 half steps + 4 half steps (7 half steps above root)
Augmented =	Root position + 4 half steps + 4 half steps (8 half steps above root)
Diminished =	Root position + 3 half steps + 3 half steps (6 half steps above root)
Building Triads with Major Scale Degrees	
Major =	1, 3, 5
Minor =	1, f3, 5
Augmented =	1, 3, s5
Diminished =	1, f3, f5

Major triads

Because they're made of intervals, triads are affected by interval *quality* (see Chapter 9 for a refresher on quantity and quality). The quantities of the notes that make up the triad are intervals of root, third, and fifth, but it's the interval quality of each note that changes the voicing of the triad.

A major triad contains a root, a major third above the root, and a perfect fifth above the root. You can build major triads in two ways. We describe each method in the following sections.

Half-step counting method

You can count out the half steps between notes to build a major triad using this formula:

Root position + 4 half steps + 3 half steps (or 7 half steps above root)

Figure 10-6 shows C major on the piano keyboard. The pattern stays the same no matter the root, but it looks trickier when you move away from C. Notice the pattern of half steps between the root, the third, and the fifth.

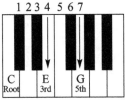

Figure 10-6: C major on the keyboard.

© John Wiley & Sons, Inc.

First, major third, and fifth method

The second way to construct major triads is to simply take the first, third, and fifth notes from a major scale.

For example, if someone asks you to write down an F major chord, you first write out the key signature for F major, as shown in Figure 10-7. (See Chapter 8 for more on key signatures.)

Figure 10-7:
The key
signature for
F major.

© John Wiley & Sons, Inc.

Then you write your triad on the staff, using F as your root, as seen in Figure 10-8.

Figure 10-8:
Add the F
major triad.

© John Wiley & Sons, Inc.

If you were to build an A flat major chord, you would first write down the key signature for A flat major and then build the triad, as shown in Figure 10-9.

Figure 10-9:
The A flat
major triad.

© John Wiley & Sons, Inc.

Minor triads

A minor triad is made up of a root, a minor third above the root, and a perfect fifth above the root. As with major triads, you can build minor triads two different ways, as we note in the following sections.

Half-step counting method

As with major triads (see earlier section), you can count out the half steps between notes to build a minor chord using this formula:

Root position + 3 half steps + 4 half steps (7 half steps above root)

Figure 10-10 shows C minor on the piano keyboard, and Figure 10-11 shows it on the staff. In Figure 10-10, notice the pattern of half steps between the root, the third, and the fifth.

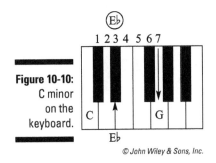

Figure 10-10:
C minor
on the
keyboard.

© John Wiley & Sons, Inc.

Figure 10-11:
C minor on
the staff.

© John Wiley & Sons, Inc.

First, minor third, and fifth method

The second way to construct minor triads is to just take the first, the minor or *flat third* (which means you lower the third degree of the major third one half step), and fifth intervals from a major scale.

For example, for an F minor chord, you write down the key signature for F major and then build the triad, as in Figure 10-12.

Figure 10-12:
The F minor
triad lowers
the third one
half step.

© John Wiley & Sons, Inc.

If you were to build an A flat minor chord, you would write the A flat key signature and add the notes, flatting the third, as shown in Figure 10-13.

Figure 10-13:
The A flat minor triad lowers the third one half step.

© John Wiley & Sons, Inc.

Augmented triads

Augmented triads are major triads that have had the fifth raised a half step, creating a slightly dissonant sound.

An augmented triad is a stack of major thirds with four half steps between each interval.

You can build a C augmented triad (written as *Caug*) by counting out the half steps between intervals, like this:

Root position + 4 half steps + 4 half steps (8 half steps above root)

C augmented is shown in Figures 10-14 and 10-15.

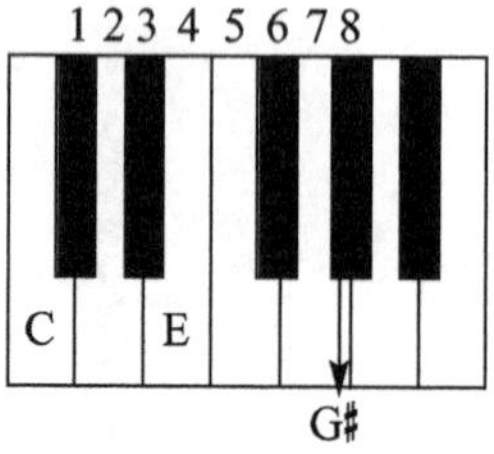

Figure 10-14:
C augmented on the keyboard.

1 2 3 4 5 6 7 8

C   E

G♯

© John Wiley & Sons, Inc.

Figure 10-15:
C augmented on the staff.

© John Wiley & Sons, Inc.

Using the method of starting with the major key signature first and then building the chord, the formula you want to remember for building augmented chords is

Augmented triad = 1 + 3 + sharp 5

So the first major scale degree and third major scale degree stay the same in the chord, but the fifth major scale degree is raised a half step.

It's important to note here that *sharp 5* doesn't mean that the note will necessarily be a sharp. Instead, it means that the fifth note occurring in the scale degree is raised, or sharped, a half step.

Therefore, if someone asks you to write down an augmented F triad, you first write the key signature for F and then write your triad on the staff, using F as your root and raising the fifth position one half step, as shown in Figure 10-16.

Figure 10-16:
The F
augmented
triad.

© John Wiley & Sons, Inc.

If you were to build an A flat augmented triad, you would go through the same process and come up with a triad that looks like the one in Figure 10-17. Note that the perfect fifth of A flat major is an E flat. Given A flat's key signature, you have to "natural" the fifth to get to that E natural.

Figure 10-17:
The A flat
augmented
triad.

© John Wiley & Sons, Inc.

Diminished triads

Diminished triads are minor triads that have had the fifth lowered a half step.

Diminished triads are stacks of minor thirds with three half steps between each interval.

You can build a C diminished triad (written as *Cdim*) by counting out the half steps between intervals, like this:

Root position + 3 half steps + 3 half steps (6 half steps above root)

C diminished is shown in Figures 10-18 and 10-19.

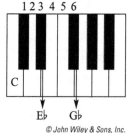

Figure 10-18:
C diminished on the keyboard.

© John Wiley & Sons, Inc.

Figure 10-19:
C diminished on the staff.

© John Wiley & Sons, Inc.

Using the method of starting with the major key signature first and then building the chord, the formula you want to remember for building diminished chords is

Diminished triad = 1 + flat 3 + flat 5

So the first major scale degree stays the same, but the third major scale degree and the fifth major scale degree are both lowered one half step.

It's important to note here that the terms *flat 3* and *flat 5* don't mean these notes will necessarily *be* flats. These notes are only the third and fifth notes occurring in the scale degree lowered a half step.

Therefore, if someone asks you to write down an F diminished triad, you first write the key signature for F, and then you write your triad on the staff, using F as your root and lowering the third and fifth intervals one half step, as shown in Figure 10-20.

Figure 10-20:
The F
diminished
triad.

© John Wiley & Sons, Inc.

If you were to build an A flat diminished triad, you would go through the same process and come up with a triad that looks like the one in Figure 10-21.

Figure 10-21:
The A flat
diminished
triad.

© John Wiley & Sons, Inc.

Note that the perfect fifth of A flat major is an E flat — flatting the fifth makes it a double flat.

Expanding to Seventh Chords

When you add another third above the fifth of a triad, you've gone beyond the land of triads. You now have a *seventh chord.* Seventh chords got their name because the last third interval is a seventh interval above the root.

Several kinds of seventh chords exist. The six most commonly used seventh chords are as follows:

- Major sevenths
- Minor sevenths
- Dominant sevenths
- Minor 7 flat 5 chords (also sometimes called *half-diminished*)
- Diminished sevenths
- Minor-major sevenths

The easiest way to understand how sevenths are built is to think of each as a triad with a seventh tacked onto it. Looking at sevenths this way, you can see that seventh chords are really just variations on the four triads discussed earlier in this chapter. The names of the chords tell you how to put the seventh together with the triad.

The following sections walk you through building a variety of different sevenths: major, minor, dominant, diminished, and more. Table 10-2 gathers all this info on how to build sevenths.

Table 10-2	Building Sevenths
Building Sevenths by Counting Half Steps	
Major =	Root + 4 half steps + 3 half steps + 4 half steps (11 half steps above root)
Minor =	Root + 3 half steps + 4 half steps + 3 half steps (10 half steps above root)
Dominant =	Root + 4 half steps + 3 half steps + 3 half steps (10 half steps above root)
Minor 7 flat 5 =	Root + 3 half steps + 3 half steps + 4 half steps (10 half steps above root)
Diminished =	Root + 3 half steps + 3 half steps + 3 half steps (9 half steps above root)
Minor-major =	Root + 3 half steps + 4 half steps + 4 half steps (11 half steps above root)
Building Sevenths with Major Scale Degrees	
Major =	1, 3, 5, 7
Minor =	1, ♭3, 5, ♭7
Dominant =	1, 3, 5, ♭7
Minor 7 flat 5 =	1, ♭3, f5, ♭7
Diminished =	1, ♭3, f5, ♭7
Minor-major =	1, ♭3, 5, 7

Major sevenths

A major seventh chord consists of a major triad with a major seventh added above the root. Figure 10-22 shows how to first build a major triad using the C major example from earlier in the chapter.

Figure 10-22:
C major
triad.

© John Wiley & Sons, Inc.

Now add a major seventh to the top of the pile, as is done in Figure 10-23. The result is

C major seventh = C major triad + major seventh interval

Figure 10-23:
C major
seventh
(CM7 or
Cmaj7).

© John Wiley & Sons, Inc.

B natural is a major seventh from the root of the triad. Notice that it's also a major third (four half steps) away from the fifth of the triad.

Minor sevenths

A minor seventh chord consists of a minor triad with a minor seventh added above the root. Using the C minor example from earlier in the chapter, you first build a minor triad like the one in Figure 10-24.

Figure 10-24:
C minor triad
(Cm or Cmi).

© John Wiley & Sons, Inc.

Now add a minor seventh to the top of the pile, as is done in Figure 10-25. The result is

C minor seventh = C minor triad + minor seventh

Figure 10-25:
C minor
seventh
(Cm7).

© John Wiley & Sons, Inc.

B flat is a minor seventh (ten half steps) from the root of the triad. It's also a minor third (three half steps) away from the fifth of the triad.

To build a minor seventh using major scale degrees, you pick the first, flatted third, fifth, and flatted seventh degrees from the scale.

Dominant sevenths

A dominant seventh chord, sometimes called a *major-minor* seventh chord, consists of a major triad with a minor seventh added above the root, as shown in Figure 10-26. The formula for this seventh is

C dominant seventh = C major triad + minor seventh

Figure 10-26:
C dominant
seventh
(C7).

© John Wiley & Sons, Inc.

Ten half steps fall between the root and the minor seventh, and three half steps fall between the fifth of the triad and the minor seventh.

The dominant seventh is the only seventh chord that doesn't truly give away the relationship between the triad and the seventh in its name. You just have to remember it. And don't confuse major seventh and dominant seventh chords. The major seventh is always written as M7, whereas the dominant seventh is written simply as 7 (occasionally, dom7). For example, G major seventh is written GM7, and the dominant is written G7.

To build a dominant seventh using major scale degrees, you pick the first, third, fifth, and flatted seventh degrees from the scale.

Minor 7 flat 5 chords

A *minor 7 flat 5 chord* (or *half-diminished seventh*) is a diminished triad with a minor seventh added above the root. Its name, minor 7 flat 5, tells you everything you need to know about how this chord is supposed to be put together.

Minor 7 refers to the seventh being a minor seventh, or ten half steps, from the root, as shown in Figure 10-27.

Figure 10-27:
The root and minor seventh of a C minor 7 flat 5 chord.

© John Wiley & Sons, Inc.

Flat 5 refers to the diminished triad, which shares a flatted third with a minor chord but also has a flatted fifth, as shown in Figure 10-28.

Figure 10-28:
C diminished triad.

© John Wiley & Sons, Inc.

Put the two together, and you have the C minor 7 flat 5 (half-diminished) chord, as shown in Figure 10-29.

Figure 10-29:
C minor 7 flat 5 chord.

© John Wiley & Sons, Inc.

To build a minor 7 flat 5 (half-diminished) chord using major scale degrees, you pick the first, flatted third, flatted fifth, and flatted seventh degrees from the scale.

Diminished sevenths

The *diminished seventh* chord is a stack of three consecutive minor thirds. The name is also is a dead giveaway on how the chord is to be built. Just as with the major seventh, which is a major triad with a major seventh, and the minor seventh, which is a minor triad with a minor seventh, a diminished seventh is a diminished triad with a diminished seventh from the root tacked onto it. You can see a diminished seventh in Figure 10-30. The formula for the diminished seventh is as follows:

C diminished seventh = C diminished triad + diminished seventh

Figure 10-30: C diminished seventh (Cdim7).

© John Wiley & Sons, Inc.

Note that the seventh in a diminished seventh is *double-flatted* from the major seventh, so the diminished seventh of Cdim7 is a double-flatted B. Just as with intervals, though, spelling counts — no matter what accidentals appear, a C seventh chord has to have some form of C, E, G, and B.

To build a diminished seventh using major scale degrees, you pick the first, flatted third, flatted fifth, and double-flatted seventh degrees from the scale.

Minor-major sevenths

The name *minor-major sevenths* isn't supposed to be confusing. The first part of the name tells you that the first part of the chord, the triad, is a minor chord, and the second part of the name tells you that the second part of the chord, the seventh, is a major seventh above the root.

Therefore, to build a minor-major seventh chord, start with your minor chord, as shown in Figure 10-31.

Figure 10-31: C minor triad.

© John Wiley & Sons, Inc.

Then add your major seventh, as in Figure 10-32. The formula is as follows:

C minor-major seventh = C minor + major seventh interval

Figure 10-32:
C minor-
major
seventh
(Cm/M7).

© John Wiley & Sons, Inc.

To build a minor-major seventh using major scale degrees, you pick the first, flatted third, fifth, and seventh degrees from the scale.

Looking at All the Triads and Sevenths

This section lays out all the types of triads and sevenths we discuss in this chapter in order of appearance and for every key. Figures 10-33 through 10-47 illustrate the triads and sevenths. You can also check out Audio Tracks 67 through 81 to hear the triads and sevenths in action.

A

Play Track 67 to hear the triads and sevenths of A: A major, A minor, A augmented, A diminished, A major seventh, A minor seventh, A dominant seventh, A minor 7 flat 5, A diminished seventh, and A minor-major seventh.

Track 67

Figure 10-33:
A triads and
sevenths.

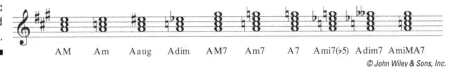

AM   Am   Aaug   Adim   AM7   Am7   A7   Ami7(♭5) Adim7 AmiMA7

© John Wiley & Sons, Inc.

A flat

Play Track 68 to hear the triads and sevenths of A flat: A flat major, A flat minor, A flat augmented, A flat diminished, A flat major seventh, A flat minor seventh, A flat dominant seventh, A flat minor 7 flat 5, A flat diminished seventh, and A flat minor-major seventh.

Track 68

Figure 10-34:
A flat triads and sevenths.

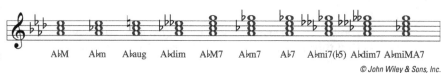

A♭M   A♭m   A♭aug   A♭dim   A♭M7   A♭m7   A♭7   A♭mi7(♭5)   A♭dim7   A♭miMA7

© John Wiley & Sons, Inc.

B

Play Track 69 to hear the triads and sevenths of B: B major, B minor, B augmented, B diminished, B major seventh, B minor seventh, B dominant seventh, B minor 7 flat 5, B diminished seventh, and B minor-major seventh.

Track 69

Figure 10-35:
B triads and sevenths.

BM   Bm   Baug   Bdim   BM7   Bm7   B7   Bmi7(♭5)   Bdim7   BmiMA7

© John Wiley & Sons, Inc.

B flat

Play Track 70 to hear the triads and sevenths of B flat: B flat major, B flat minor, B flat augmented, B flat diminished, B flat major seventh, B flat minor seventh, B flat dominant seventh, B flat minor 7 flat 5, B flat diminished seventh, and B flat minor-major seventh.

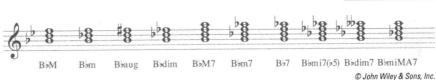

Figure 10-36: B flat triads and sevenths.

B♭M B♭m B♭aug B♭dim B♭M7 B♭m7 B♭7 B♭mi7(♭5) B♭dim7 B♭miMA7

C

Play Track 71 to hear the triads and sevenths of C: C major, C minor, C augmented, C diminished, C major seventh, C minor seventh, C dominant seventh, C minor 7 flat 5, C diminished seventh, and C minor-major seventh.

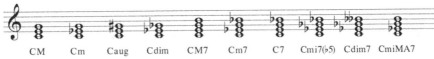

Figure 10-37: C triads and sevenths.

CM Cm Caug Cdim CM7 Cm7 C7 Cmi7(♭5) Cdim7 CmiMA7

C flat

Play Track 72 to hear the triads and sevenths of C flat: C flat major, C flat minor, C flat augmented, C flat diminished, C flat major seventh, C flat minor seventh, C flat dominant seventh, C flat minor 7 flat 5, C flat diminished seventh, and C flat minor-major seventh.

Note: C flat is an enharmonic equivalent of B. The chords here sound exactly like the B chords, but in the interest of being complete, we include C flat as well.

Figure 10-38: C flat triads and sevenths.

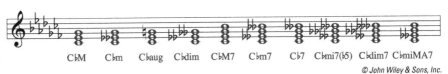

C♭M C♭m C♭aug C♭dim C♭M7 C♭m7 C♭7 C♭mi7(♭5) C♭dim7 C♭miMA7

C sharp

Play Track 73 to hear the triads and sevenths of C sharp: C sharp major, C sharp minor, C sharp augmented, C sharp diminished, C sharp major seventh, C sharp minor seventh, C sharp dominant seventh, C sharp minor 7 flat 5, C sharp diminished seventh, and C sharp minor-major seventh.

Track 73

Figure 10-39:
C sharp triads and sevenths.

C#M   C#m   C#aug   C#dim   C#M7   C#m7   C#7   C#mi7(♭5)   C#dim7   C#miMA7

© John Wiley & Sons, Inc.

D

Play Track 74 to hear the triads and sevenths of D: D major, D minor, D augmented, D diminished, D major seventh, D minor seventh, D dominant seventh, D minor 7 flat 5, D diminished seventh, and D minor-major seventh.

Track 74

Figure 10-40:
D triads and sevenths.

DM   Dm   Daug   Ddim   DM7   Dm7   D7   Dmi7(♭5)   Ddim7   DmiMA7

© John Wiley & Sons, Inc.

D flat

Play Track 75 to hear the triads and sevenths of D flat: D flat major, D flat minor, D flat augmented, D flat diminished, D flat major seventh, D flat minor seventh, D flat dominant seventh, D flat minor 7 flat 5, D flat diminished seventh, and D flat minor-major seventh.

Figure 10-41:
D flat
triads and
sevenths.

DbM   Dbm   Dbaug   Dbdim   DbM7   Dbm7   Db7   Dbmi7(b5)   Dbdim7   DbmiMA7

© John Wiley & Sons, Inc.

E

Play Track 76 to hear the triads and sevenths of E: E major, E minor, E augmented, E diminished, E major seventh, E minor seventh, E dominant seventh, E minor 7 flat 5, E diminished seventh, and E minor-major seventh.

Track 76

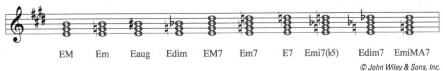

Figure 10-42:
E triads and
sevenths.

EM   Em   Eaug   Edim   EM7   Em7   E7   Emi7(b5)   Edim7   EmiMA7

© John Wiley & Sons, Inc.

E flat

Play Track 77 to hear the triads and sevenths of E flat: E flat major, E flat minor, E flat augmented, E flat diminished, E flat major seventh, E flat minor seventh, E flat dominant seventh, E flat minor 7 flat 5, E flat diminished seventh, and E flat minor-major seventh.

Track 77

Figure 10-43:
E flat
triads and
sevenths.

EbM   Ebm   Ebaug   Ebdim   EbM7   Ebm7   Eb7   Ebmi7(b5)   Ebdim7   EbmiMA7

© John Wiley & Sons, Inc.

F

Play Track 78 to hear the triads and sevenths of F: F major, F minor, F augmented, F diminished, F major seventh, F minor seventh, F dominant seventh, F minor 7 flat 5, F diminished seventh, and F minor-major seventh.

Track 78

Figure 10-44:
F triads and sevenths.

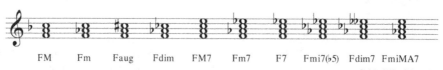

FM   Fm   Faug   Fdim   FM7   Fm7   F7   Fmi7(♭5)   Fdim7   FmiMA7

© John Wiley & Sons, Inc.

F sharp

Play Track 79 to hear the triads and sevenths of F sharp: F sharp major, F sharp minor, F sharp augmented, F sharp diminished, F sharp major seventh, F sharp minor seventh, F sharp dominant seventh, F sharp minor 7 flat 5, F sharp diminished seventh, and F sharp minor-major seventh.

Track 79

Figure 10-45:
F sharp triads and sevenths.

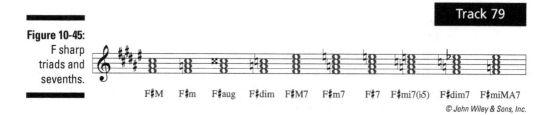

F♯M   F♯m   F♯aug   F♯dim   F♯M7   F♯m7   F♯7   F♯mi7(♭5)   F♯dim7   F♯miMA7

© John Wiley & Sons, Inc.

G

Play Track 80 to hear the triads and sevenths of G: G major, G minor, G augmented, G diminished, G major seventh, G minor seventh, G dominant seventh, G minor 7 flat 5, G diminished seventh, and G minor-major seventh.

Track 80

Figure 10-46:
G triads and
sevenths.

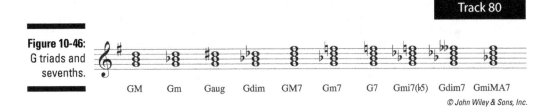

GM Gm Gaug Gdim GM7 Gm7 G7 Gmi7(♭5) Gdim7 GmiMA7

© John Wiley & Sons, Inc.

G flat

Play Track 81 to hear the triads and sevenths of G flat: G flat major, G flat minor, G flat augmented, G flat diminished, G flat major seventh, G flat minor seventh, G flat dominant seventh, G flat minor 7 flat 5, G flat diminished seventh, and G flat minor-major seventh.

Track 81

Figure 10-47:
G flat
triads and
sevenths.

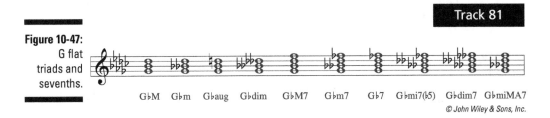

G♭M G♭m G♭aug G♭dim G♭M7 G♭m7 G♭7 G♭mi7(♭5) G♭dim7 G♭miMA7

© John Wiley & Sons, Inc.

Manipulating Triads through Voicing and Inversion

Here's a riddle: When is a triad not a perfect little stack of thirds built on top of a root? Answer: When its *voicing* is *open,* or when it's *inverted. Voicing,* or *spacing* as it's referred to in some classical circles, simply refers to the way a chord is arranged. We go into more detail about voicing and inversion in the following sections.

Taking a look at open and close voicing

Sometimes, the notes of a triad are spread out over two or more octaves, with the different parts rearranged so that, for example, the root may carry the highest-sounding note, or the third, or the fifth can carry the lowest-sounding note. The notes are still the same (C, E, G, for example) — they're just located an octave or even octaves above or below where you would expect them in a normal triad. When all the notes of a chord are in the same octave, the chord is considered to be in a *close voicing*.

Figure 10-48 shows a C major chord with close voicing.

Figure 10-48:
C major chord with close voicing.

© John Wiley & Sons, Inc.

The chord in Figure 10-49, however, is also a C major chord, but with *open voicing*, meaning that the notes in the chord aren't all located in the same octave.

Figure 10-49:
C major chord with open voicing.

© John Wiley & Sons, Inc.

Both chords in Figures 10-48 and 10-49 have the same notes contained in the triad, but in the latter case the third has been raised a full octave from its close position. Both chords are still considered to be in the *root position*, because the root note, C, is still the lowest note of the triad.

Identifying inverted chords

If the lowest-sounding pitch of a chord is *not* the root, the chord is considered to be *inverted*. Here are the possible inversions of a triad:

- ✓ **First inversion:** If the third of a chord is the lowest-sounding note, the chord is in *first inversion*. Figure 10-50 shows the C major chord in first inversion, with close (same octave) and open (different octaves) voicing.

✔ **Second inversion:** When the fifth of a chord is the lowest-sounding note, the chord is in *second inversion*. Figure 10-51 shows the C major chord in second inversion.

✔ **Third inversion:** When the seventh of a chord is the lowest-sounding note, that chord is in *third inversion*. Figure 10-52 shows the C major 7 chord in third inversion.

Figure 10-50:
C major chord in first inversion, close and open voicing.

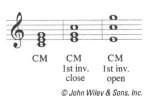

CM   CM   CM
1st inv. 1st inv.
close   open

© John Wiley & Sons, Inc.

Figure 10-51:
C major chord in second inversion, close and open voicing.

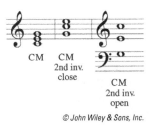

CM   CM
2nd inv.
close

CM
2nd inv.
open

© John Wiley & Sons, Inc.

Figure 10-52:
C major 7 chord in third inversion, close and open voicing.

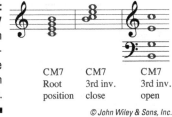

CM7   CM7   CM7
Root   3rd inv. 3rd inv.
position close   open

© John Wiley & Sons, Inc.

So how do you identify inverted chords? Simple: They aren't arranged in stacks of thirds. To find out which chord it is, you have to rearrange the chord into thirds again. Only one way exists to rearrange a chord into thirds, so you don't have to guess on the order of the notes. You may need a little patience, though.

Look at, for instance, the three inverted chords shown in Figure 10-53.

Figure 10-53:
Inverted
chords.

© John Wiley & Sons, Inc.

If you try moving the notes up or down octaves (in order to rearrange them so they're all in stacks of thirds), they end up being an F sharp major triad, a G diminished seventh, and a D major triad (see Figure 10-54).

Figure 10-54:
Rearranging
the inverted
chords into
stacks of
thirds.

F♯M   Gdim7 DM

© John Wiley & Sons, Inc.

From rearranging the chords, you can tell that the first example was an F sharp major in second inversion, because the fifth was the lowest-sounding note in the chord. The second example was a G diminished seventh, also in second inversion, because the fifth of the chord was at the bottom of the stack. The third example was a D major triad in first inversion, because the third of the chord was the lowest-sounding note.

Doubling the fun

In addition the methods we preview in this chapter, you also can build a chord through *doubling*, which simply means you have multiple versions of the root, third, fifth, or even seventh in a chord. For example, a C major triad is still a C major triad with two C's in it, as long as it has at least one E and G. It's also still a C major triad if it has multiple E's or G's; however, doubling the root note is the most common use of doubling.

Exploring Extended Chords

The most commonly used chords in Western music are triads, which are constructed of stacked thirds. Triads are made up of the first (root), third, and fifth degree of a scale. If you add one more note, you have a seventh, which is a chord made up of the first, third, fifth, and seventh scale degrees. But it doesn't stop there! You can continue to make bigger and bigger chords by adding even more thirds to the stack, until either you literally have no more keys left on the piano to work with (or strings on the guitar) or you run out of fingers. These bigger and more complex chords built from stacked thirds are called *extended chords*.

Just like when you're constructing triads and seventh chords (see the sections earlier in this chapter), the quantity of each chord built on a scale remains the same, but the quality or the chord changes depending on which notes in the chord are raised or lowered a half-step from its major scale degree. (For more on quantity and quality, see Chapter 9.)

One thing to realize when you're building extended chords is that you can find many more possible permutations out there. To keep things from getting too ridiculous, though, we're just going to give you a few examples to work with.

Curious about all the potential extended chords? Think of it like a combination lock: When you have three notes to work with, as in triads, you have only four different ways to construct a chord: major, minor, augmented, and diminished. When you're working with seventh chords, we've shown you six ways to construct chords: major seventh, minor seventh, flatted seventh, minor seventh, diminished seventh, and minor-major seventh. When you add one, two, or three more notes to the mix, you have even more possibilities available to you.

Because this book isn't just about building chords, we limit ourselves in the following sections to the most commonly used permutations of extended chords, concentrating more on the ninth chords, which are used pretty extensively in pop and jazz music. We also highlight just a couple of eleventh and thirteenth chords, since most people have hands smaller than Fats Waller's and have trouble covering all the notes.

Ninth chords

A *ninth chord* is a chord that has one more third added to it than a seventh chord, and results in a bigger, fuller sound than even a triad or seventh chord. So, for example, a C9M, consisting of the first, third, fifth, seventh, and ninth degree of the C major scale, is just our CM7 chord from Figure 10-37, with one more third stuck on top of the pile. The result is the CM9 chord, which you can see in Figure 10-55.

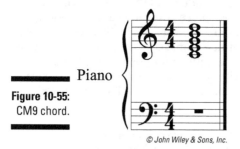

Piano

Figure 10-55:
CM9 chord.

© John Wiley & Sons, Inc.

A ninth chord is formed by combining the first (root), third, fifth, flatted seventh, and ninth degrees of a major scale, and is written by adding a major third to a dominant seventh chord For example, in the C major scale, you write C9. So, if we were to construct ninth chords for every major scale in the Circle of Fifths, it would look like the chords found in Figure 10-56. (For more on the Circle of Fifths, go to Chapter 8.)

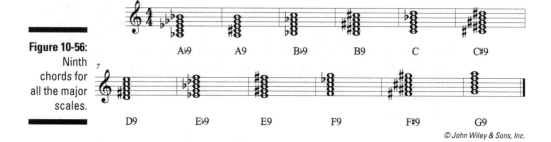

Figure 10-56:
Ninth
chords for
all the major
scales.

© John Wiley & Sons, Inc.

Minor ninth chords

Minor ninth chords are formed by combining the first, flatted third, fifth, flatted seventh, and ninth degrees of a major scale, or a Minor Seventh chord with a major ninth added. The symbol you use is min9, mi9, m9, or -9. So, for example, C minor 9 would be written as either Cmin9, Cmi9, Cm9, or C-9, depending on the transcriber. If we were to construct minor ninth chords for every major scale, following the Circle of Fifths, the result would look like Figure 10-57.

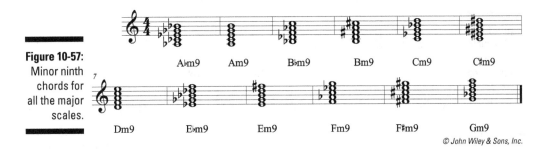

Figure 10-57:
Minor ninth chords for all the major scales.

Major ninth chords

Major ninth chords are formed by combining the first, third, fifth, major seventh, and ninth degrees of a major scale — or by adding a major ninth to a Major Seventh chord — and is written as Ma9, or M9. Check out Figure 10-58 to see what it would look like if we constructed major ninth chords for every major scale, in order of the Circle of Fifths.

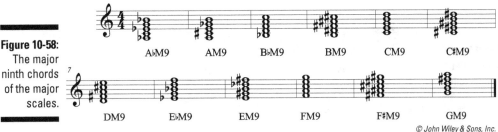

Figure 10-58:
The major ninth chords of the major scales.

Ninth augmented fifth chords

Ninth augmented fifth chords are formed by combining the first, third, sharped fifth, flatted seventh, and ninth degrees of a major scale, and is written as 9♯5, as in C9♯5. Wondering what it would look like if we constructed ninth augmented fifth chords for every major scale? Well, wonder no more. Figure 10-59 shows you the ninth augmented fifth chords, following the Circle of Fifths.

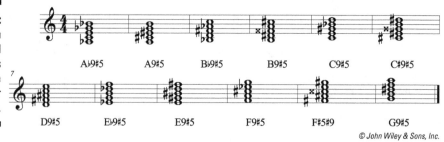

Figure 10-59: The ninth augmented fifth chords in all the major scales.

© John Wiley & Sons, Inc.

Ninth flatted fifth chord

You form ninth flatted fifth chords by combining the first, third, flatted fifth, flatted seventh, and ninth degrees of the major scale. When you're writing a ninth flatted fifth for a particular scale, you add 9♭5. For example, the chord C ninth flatted fifth is written C9♭5 or C9-5. Figure 10-60 shows what it would look like if we were to construct ninth flatted fifth chords for every major scale, following the Circle of Fifths.

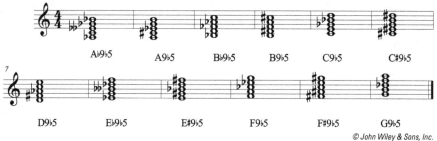

Figure 10-60: Ninth flatted fifth chords for every major scale.

© John Wiley & Sons, Inc.

Seventh flat ninth piano chords

When you combine the first, third, fifth, flatted seventh, and flatted ninth degrees of the major scale, or take a C7 chord and add a diminished ninth to it, you get a seventh flat ninth chord. You write a seventh flat ninth piano chord as 7-9 or 7♭9, as in C7-9 or C7♭9. To see the seventh flat ninth chords for every major scale, check out Figure 10-61.

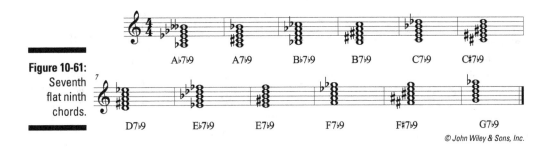

Figure 10-61:
Seventh
flat ninth
chords.

Augmented ninth chords

You can build an augmented ninth chord by combining the first, third, fifth, flatted seventh, and sharped ninth degrees of a chord's major scale, or a dominant seventh chord plus a major ninth. When writing it out, you would add a 9+ or 7+9 to the chord name. The C major augmented ninth chord would look like C9+ or C7+9. If we were to construct augmented ninth chords in every major scale, following the Circle of Fifths, it would look like Figure 10-62.

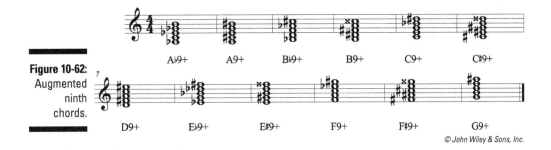

Figure 10-62:
Augmented
ninth
chords.

Eleventh chords

Just as a ninth chord is created when you stack five thirds on top of one another (see preceding sections), an eleventh chord is formed when you have a stack of six thirds. Many, many permutations of eleventh chords are possible, but since they're rarely used, the only two we're going to cover are eleventh chords and augmented eleventh chords.

You can create an eleventh chord when you combine the first, third, fifth, flatted seventh, ninth, and eleventh of the major scale. You indicate an eleventh chord by writing 11 after the scale, such as C11 for the C major scale. Check out Figure 10-63 to see some examples of eleventh chords.

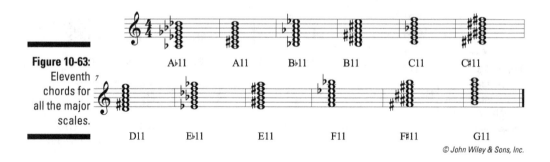

Figure 10-63:
Eleventh chords for all the major scales.

© John Wiley & Sons, Inc.

To build an augmented eleventh chord, you combine the first, third, fifth, flatted seventh, ninth, and sharped eleventh of the major scale. When writing out an augmented eleventh chord, you add either 11+ or 7aug11 to the chord name, as in C11+ or C7aug11 for the C major scale. See Figure 10-64 for augmented eleventh chords of all the major scales.

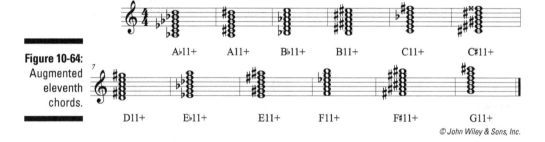

Figure 10-64:
Augmented eleventh chords.

© John Wiley & Sons, Inc.

Thirteenth chords

Here we cover just three of the most-common arrangements of the thirteenth chord: the thirteenth chord, the thirteenth flat nine chord, and the thirteenth flat ninth flat fifth chord. We focus on these three because these are the three you are most likely come across, because they are probably the most harmonious of the dozens of possibilities.

The more thirds you stack together in a chord, the bigger the chance of ending up with a dissonant-sounding chord. In fact, many musicians consider thirteenth (and beyond) chords as merely theoretical chords, in that they know they exist, they know how to build them, but they're never going to use them when writing or playing a piece of music.

A thirteenth chord is a stack of seven thirds: the first, third, fifth, flat seventh, ninth, eleventh, and thirteenth degrees of the major scale, or a C11 with one more major third on top. Writing it out for the scales is pretty simple. All you do is add the number 13 to the scale. So, C13 would indicate a thirteenth chord in the C major scale. Figure 10-65 contains all the thirteenth chords of the major scales.

Figure 10-65:
Thirteenth chords.

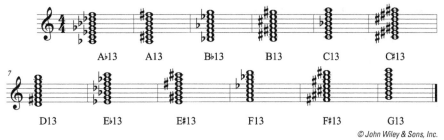

© John Wiley & Sons, Inc.

A thirteenth flat nine chord is made up of the first, third, fifth, flatted seventh, flatted ninth, eleventh, and thirteenth degrees of a major scale and is written as 13♭9, as in C13♭9 for the C major scale. See Figure 10-66 for all the possible thirteenth flat nine chords.

Figure 10-66:
Thirteenth flat nine chords.

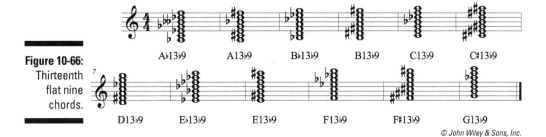

© John Wiley & Sons, Inc.

A thirteenth flat ninth flat fifth chord is made up of the first, third, flatted fifth, flatted seventh, flatted ninth, eleventh, and thirteenth degrees of a major scale. You can write it out as 13(♭9, ♭5), as in C13(♭9, ♭5) for the C major scale. Figure 10-67 shows all the possible thirteenth flat ninth flat fifth chords.

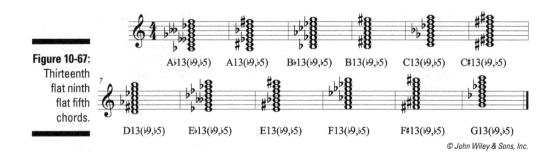

Figure 10-67:
Thirteenth
flat ninth
flat fifth
chords.

Ab13(b9,b5) A13(b9,b5) Bb13(b9,b5) B13(b9,b5) C13(b9,b5) C#13(b9,b5)

D13(b9,b5) Eb13(b9,b5) E13(b9,b5) F13(b9,b5) F#13(b9,b5) G13(b9,b5)

Chapter 11

Chord Progressions

*A*s you may have guessed, constructing music is about as far from randomly throwing notes together as writing a book is from randomly pulling letters out of a Scrabble bag. You can find about as many rules to putting a song together as you can to putting a sentence together, and in this chapter we show you a few more.

When you analyze the bulk of Western harmonic music, you start to see certain patterns emerge in the ways chord progressions are built. It's possible for any one chord to progress to any one of the other chords in a key; however, certain chord progressions are used more frequently than others. Why? Because they simply sound better. These progressions obviously are natural patterns that are pleasing to listeners and composers alike, because the same patterns continuously appear in popular music, classical, rock, jazz, and so on.

Music theorists have taken note of these patterns and have come up with a set of rules concerning chord progressions. These rules, which we discuss throughout this chapter, are immensely helpful in songwriting.

Reviewing Diatonic Chords, Chromatic Chords, and Minor Scale Modes

In Western music, the key signature tells you which notes can be used in that piece. Therefore, if you have a song written in C major, the only seven notes that can appear (in any order) in the song are C, D, E, F, G, A, and B (with the odd sharp or flat thrown in as rare exceptions allowed by accidentals).

If your song is written in A major, the only notes appearing in that song will be A, B, C sharp, D, E, F sharp, and G sharp (again, with possible accidentals). The chords will also be made of some combination of these seven notes for each key.

Chords built on the seven notes of a major key signature are called *diatonic chords.* Chords that are built on notes *outside* the key signature are called *chromatic chords.*

Minor keys get a little trickier because nine notes can potentially fit under a single minor key signature when you consider the melodic and harmonic minor scales (review Chapter 7 if you're unclear on these kinds of minor scales).

Because the natural, melodic, and harmonic scales are taught as separate scales, musicians often have the misconception that you must stick to only one of these types of minor scales when composing music. Alas, for those folks who like nice, simple rules to build music against, this just isn't so.

The easiest way to think about chords built on minor keys is to recognize that each key signature has just one minor scale. One facet of minor keys is the flexible nature of the 6th and 7th degrees of the scale.

The 6th and 7th degrees can be in the scale in two different ways depending on what sounds better in the context of the music. Often the two different versions of those degrees, or *modes,* will appear in the same piece of music. The minor scale therefore has potentially nine notes in it, as shown in Figure 11-1.

Figure 11-1:
The A minor scale, including harmonic and melodic mode steps.

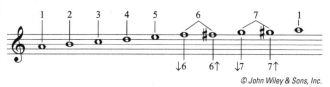

© *John Wiley & Sons, Inc.*

Notice how the use of arrows indicates where the 6th and 7th degrees are either raised (up arrow) or unaltered (down arrow).

Identifying and Naming Chord Progressions

Triads strung together to form a succession of chords are called *progressions*. Chord progressions make up pretty much all of Western harmonic music. (You can read more about triads in Chapter 10.)

When breaking down a piece of music based on chord progressions, roman numerals represent the different scale degrees. Capitalized roman numerals represent the chords with a major third, and lowercased roman numerals represent the minor chords. Other special characters indicate whether the chord is diminished (°) or augmented (+), as you can see in Table 11-1.

Table 11-1	Basic Chord Labels	
Chord Type	*Roman Numeral Format*	*Example*
Major	Uppercase	V
Minor	Lowercase	ii
Diminished	Lowercase with°	vii°
Augmented	Uppercase with +	III+

Assigning chord names and numbers

Because the name of a chord comes from its root note, it's only natural that the root of each chord located within a scale would also carry the scale degree with its name. In other words, a chord's name tells you what the chord is, based on the root note, whereas a chord's *number* tells you what the chord does, based on key.

For example, consider the C major scale. Each note of the C major scale is assigned a scale degree number and name, like so:

Scale Degree Number and Name	Note
1 Tonic	C
2 Supertonic	D
3 Mediant	E
4 Subdominant	F
5 Dominant	G
6 Submediant	A
7 Leading tone	B
8/1 Tonic	C

When you build triads within the C major scale, each triad is assigned the scale degree of the root in its name, as shown in Figure 11-2.

Figure 11-2:
Tonic triads
in the C
major scale.

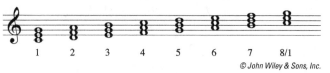

1   2   3   4   5   6   7   8/1

© John Wiley & Sons, Inc.

Looking at chord progressions in major keys

The chart for chord progressions in the C major scale looks like this:

Scale Degree Number/Name	Note
I Tonic	C
ii Supertonic	D
iii Mediant	E
IV Subdominant	F
V Dominant	G
vi Submediant	A
vii° Leading tone	B
(I) Tonic	C

Because the leading tone is a diminished triad, it has the ° symbol next to its roman numeral.

Figure 11-3 takes another look at the C major scale, this time with the chords' names according to the root of each triad written underneath them (and their shorthand names, such as CM or Dm, written above them). The capital *M* in the chord's shorthand name (such as in CM) stands for major, and the lowercase *m* (such as in Em) stands for minor.

Figure 11-3:
Triads contained within the key of C major.

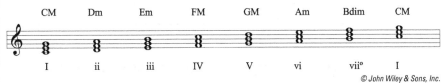

© John Wiley & Sons, Inc.

As you can see in Figure 11-3, the chord progression naturally follows the pattern of ascending the scale starting with the tonic note, in this case C. Figure 11-4 shows the triads contained within the key of E flat major. The eight notes that make up the key of E flat major are used to produce the eight chords shown in Figure 11-4.

Figure 11-4:
Triads contained within the key of E flat major.

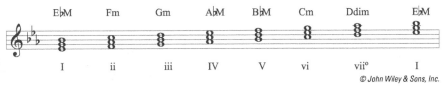

© John Wiley & Sons, Inc.

Notice that the pattern of major and minor chords is the same for C major and E flat major. In fact, it's the same for every major key. So if you say a chord is a ii chord, other musicians will automatically know that it's minor.

Table 11-2 shows common chord progressions for major keys. Any of the triads in the table with an added seventh chord are also acceptable in that triad's numbered place as well. (You can read more about seventh chords in the later section "Adding a Seventh Chord to a Triad.")

Major key signatures can contain minor chords.

Table 11-2	Common Major Key Chord Progressions
Chord	*Leads To*
I	Can appear anywhere and lead anywhere
ii	I, V, or vii° chords
iii	I, IV, or vi chords
IV	I, ii, V, or vii° chords
V	I or vi chords
vi	I, ii, iii, IV, or V chords
vii°	I chord

Checking out chord progressions in minor keys

When dealing with minor keys, the construction of triads is unfortunately a lot more involved than it is with the major keys. The 6th and 7th degrees of the scale are variable, depending on whether the music uses notes from the natural minor, harmonic minor, or melodic minor. So for nearly all minor triads, more possibilities for building chords exist in the 6th and 7th degrees than they do in the major scale. Therefore, if you're looking at a piece of music written in C minor, the possible chords within that key are the ones in Figure 11-5.

Figure 11-5:
Possible triads within the key of C minor.

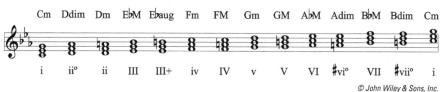

© John Wiley & Sons, Inc.

Although any of the chords from Figure 11-5 are possible, the most common choices made by traditional composers are those shown in Figure 11-6.

Notice in Figure 11-6 that the supertonic and the leading tone triads are diminished, resulting in a combination of the natural, harmonic, and melodic scales in coming up with this set of chords. Neither chord uses scale degree 6, so these two chords result from the natural and harmonic minor scales only.

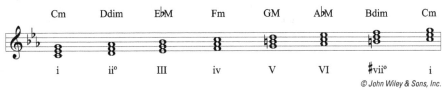

Figure 11-6:
Possible
scale
degrees
used in C
minor.

Cm   Ddim   E♭M   Fm   GM   A♭M   Bdim   Cm

i   ii°   III   iv   V   VI   ♯vii°   i

© John Wiley & Sons, Inc.

You may find it helpful to remember that, with the raised 7th degree, the 5th (V) and 7th (vii°) degrees of both major and minor scales of the same letter name are identical.

Table 11-3 shows common chord progressions for minor chords. Any of the triads in Table 11-3 with added seventh chords are also acceptable in that triad's numbered place as well. The parenthetical chords are the less-commonly used, but still acceptable, chords that would work in the progression.

Minor key signatures can contain major chords.

Table 11-3	Common Minor Key Chord Progressions
Chord	**Leads To**
i chords	Can appear anywhere and lead anywhere
ii° (ii) chords	i, V (v), or vii° (VII) chords
III (III+) chords	i, iv (IV), VI (♯vi°), or vii° (VI) chords
iv (IV) chords	i, V (v), or vii° (VII) chords
V (v) chords	I or VI (♯vi°) chords
VI (♯vi°) chords	i, III (III+), iv (IV), V (v), or vii° (VII) chords
vii° (VII) chords	i chord

Adding a Seventh Chord to a Triad

Of course, we can't forget the seventh chords (you may want to peek at Chapter 10 for a refresher on these chords). When you add the additional seventh above the regular triad, you end up with a combination of the triad's chord symbols and the seventh's symbol.

When dealing with progressions that use seventh chords, you'll see symbols like the one in Figure 11-7. This symbol indicates a *minor 7 flat 5 chord,* also sometimes called a *half-diminished seventh.*

Figure 11-7: This symbol means the chord is a minor 7 flat 5 chord (half-diminished seventh).

© John Wiley & Sons, Inc.

Table 11-4 shows the roman numerals that composers use to describe seventh chords.

Table 11-4	Seventh Chord Labels	
Seventh Chord Type	*Roman Numeral*	*Example*
Major 7th	Uppercase with M7	IM7
Major minor 7th	Uppercase with a 7	V7
Minor 7th	Lowercase with a 7	iii7
Minor 7 flat 5	Lowercase with ∅7	ii∅7
Diminished 7th	Lowercase with°	vii°

Be aware that the "M7" by the I and IV chords is common to popular music — classical musicians tend to just use a "7" for these chords. Figure 11-8 shows the seventh chords based on C major.

Figure 11-8: Sevenths in C major.

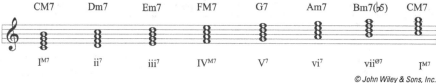

© John Wiley & Sons, Inc.

When taking into consideration the natural, harmonic, and melodic scales, 16 seventh chords can occur in a minor key. The seventh chords shown in Figure 11-9 are the most commonly used.

Figure 11-9: Seventh chords in C minor.

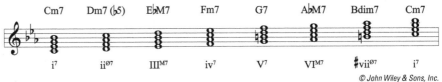

© John Wiley & Sons, Inc.

Table 11-5 collects, in one place, the major, minor, and seventh chord symbols.

Table 11-5	Major and Minor Scale Triads and Seventh Chords			
Major Scale Triads	**Minor Scale Triads**	**Rare Chords Based on Minor Scales**	**7th Chords Based on Major Scales**	**7th Chords Based on Minor Scales**
I	i		IM7	i7
ii	ii°	ii	ii7	iiø7
iii	III	III+	iii7	IIIM7
IV	iv	IV	IVM7	iv7
V	V	v	V7	V7
vi	VI	♯vi°	vi7	VIM7
vii°	♯vii°	VII	viiø7	♯vii°7

Seeing (And Hearing) Chord Progressions in Action

In this section, we show you some musical examples so you can see the rules of chord progression in practice. (You can read about these rules in the earlier section "Identifying and Naming Chord Progressions.") Note that when we talk about *chords,* we're not only talking about the stacked triads and sevenths, but we're talking about the individual notes that make up the chords as well.

Take a look at the traditional song "London Bridge," a portion of which is shown in Figure 11-10.

Figure 11-10:
First seven
measures
of "London
Bridge."

© John Wiley & Sons, Inc.

Notice that the first two measures of the song use the notes found in the
C major triad (C, E, and G), making C major the I chord. In the third measure,
the first chord is a G7 chord (G, B, D, and F). The fourth measure goes back
to the C/I chord, and returns to the G7/V chord in the seventh measure.

Judging from the common chord progression in Table 11-2, the next
chord would have to be a I or vi chord. See Figure 11-11 to find out what
happens next.

Figure 11-11:
"London
Bridge"
returns to
the I chord.

© John Wiley & Sons, Inc.

The example shown in Figure 11-12 is a lead sheet for the traditional English
folk song "Scarborough Fair." (We explain lead sheets in the next section.)
Less traditional versions of some of the chords in the minor scale are used
here: the III, IV, and VII chords. The pattern of progression still holds, though:
The i chord leads to the VII chord, the III to the IV, and then another III to the
VII chord. The I/i chord can appear anywhere in a piece of music — and, in
this one, it certainly does.

Like everything in music and art in general, you're the creator of your work,
and you can decide whether you want to follow the rules or try something
completely different. However, Tables 11-2 and 11-3 earlier in the chapter
make a good launch pad for familiarizing yourself on how chords fit against
one another. Just for fun, try playing, or just listening to, the following chord
progressions to get a feel of how easy it can be to build a great song — or at
least a halfway decent pop song.

Play Track 82 to hear the I-V-I (GM-DM-GM) chord progression in G major. Play Track 83 to hear the I-ii-V-I-iii-V-vii°-I (CM-Dm-GM-CM-Em-GM-Bdim-CM) chord progression in C major. Play Track 84 to hear the i-iv-V-VI-iv-vii°-i (Fm-Bflatm-CM-DflatM-Bflatm-Edim-Fm) chord progression in F minor.

Figure 11-12:
Lead sheet for "Scarborough Fair."

© John Wiley & Sons, Inc.

Play Track 85 to hear the i-III-VI-III-VII-i-v7-i (Am-CM-FM-CM-GM-Am-Em7-Am) chord progression in A minor.

Applying Chord Knowledge to Fake Books and Tabs

If you've ever picked up a *fake book* (thousands and thousands of these are available), you've seen lead sheets. *Lead sheets* provide just enough information for a performer to play a song competently by providing the lead melody line and noting the basic chords beneath the melody lines or above the staff to fill out the harmony, either with a straight chord or with improvisation. Figure 11-13 shows a short example.

Figure 11-13: A sample lead sheet.

© John Wiley & Sons, Inc.

Fake books are great for working on note reading and for improvising within a key. Often, for guitar fake books, the lead sheets go so far as to draw the chords for you with *tablature,* or *tabs.* Figure 11-14 shows the guitar tab for an E major chord.

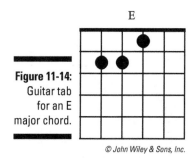

Figure 11-14: Guitar tab for an E major chord.

© John Wiley & Sons, Inc.

When reading guitar tabs, you just put your fingers on the guitar fret board where the little black dots are, and presto — you've got your chord. The lines in the figure represent the guitar strings, with the low E string on the far left. Guitar tabs in lead sheets also have the name of the chord written right next to the tab, making it even easier to either improvise or anticipate the notes that may logically be in the melody line.

Modulating to a New Key

Sometimes a piece of music temporarily moves into a new key. This move is called *modulation.* Modulation is common in traditional classical music, and long symphony and concerto movements almost always spend at least some time in a different key, usually a closely related key such as the relative minor or relative major of the original key. The key signature of these pieces of music remain the same, of course, but the qualities of and Roman numerals assigned to the chords are completely different, leading to a completely different set of chord progressions.

If you find that a piece of music suddenly contains chord progressions that you wouldn't expect in that key, it may be that the piece has modulated. Lots of accidentals in a piece or a new key signature stuck in the middle of a piece are clues that the music has modulated.

A favorite way for modulating current pop music is to simply move the key up one whole step, for example, from F major to G major (a lot of music theorists call this a "truck driver" modulation, since it feels like shifting into a higher gear). As long as you remember to keep your key signatures straight, dealing with modulation within a piece usually isn't a problem.

Reaching a Musical Cadence through Chord Progressions

A *cadence* is any place in a piece of music that has the feel of an ending. Cadence can refer to a strong, definite stopping point, like at the end of a song or even a movement or section, but it can also refer to a short pause that comes at the end of an individual musical phrase.

A piece of music can come to an end by simply stopping, of course, but if that stopping position doesn't "make sense" to the listeners, they're not going to be happy with it. Ending a song on the wrong note or notes is like ending a conversation mid-sentence, and most listeners react with dissatisfaction at a song simply stopping instead of ending properly.

A universally satisfying ending provides clues in the music, through chord progressions, that tell the listener the end of the song is near. Like the ending of a story (or a sentence, paragraph, chapter, or book), an ending in music "makes sense" if it follows certain constraints or rules. As with the customs for storytelling, these expectations can be different in different musical genres or traditions.

Of course, if you're writing music, you don't *have* to follow any of the rules of cadence, including the rules designed to provide a certain level of comfort and satisfaction for your listeners. But if you don't, be prepared for angry, torch-wielding mobs to follow you home after your performances. Don't say we didn't warn you.

The basic foundation of most music is a *harmonic goal,* where a phrase starts at a I chord and follows a series of chord progressions to end at a IV or V chord, depending on the genre (popular music tends to use the IV-I more often, and classical music uses the V-I) and the type of cadence used in the song (see Chapter 10 for more on the different types of chords). A song can have two chords or a hundred chords, and it can be a 3-second song or a 45-minute song, but, no matter what, eventually it *will* reach that harmonic goal of the IV or V chord before going back to the I chord.

A continuum of tension and release moves through music, with the I chord being the point of rest or release and every chord leading up to the return to the I chord being points of tension. The two-chord progression between the IV or V chord and the I chord is the cadence.

When you really think about it, the entire history of Western music can be summed up by I-V-I or I-IV-I. From Baroque-period music to rock 'n' roll, this formula holds darned true. What's really amazing is that this simple formula has resulted in so many songs that sound so different from one another. This variation is possible because the notes and chords in a key signature can be arranged in so many different ways.

Here are the four types of cadences commonly used in Western harmonic music:

- ✔ Authentic cadence
- ✔ Plagal cadence
- ✔ Deceptive cadence
- ✔ Half-cadence

We discuss each of these cadences in the following sections.

Authentic cadences

Authentic cadences are the most obvious-sounding cadences and are therefore considered the strongest. In an authentic cadence, the harmonic goal of the musical phrase that starts with a I/i chord and ends with a cadence is the V chord; the cadence occurs when you move from that V/v chord to a I/i chord. The phrase involved in the authentic cadence essentially ends at the V/v chord, and the song either ends completely there or starts a new phrase with the I/i chord.

Listen to Track 86 for an example of an authentic cadence.

Two types of authentic cadences are used in music:

- ✔ Perfect authentic cadence (PAC)
- ✔ Imperfect authentic cadence (IAC)

In the following sections, we provide information on each.

Perfect authentic cadence

In a *perfect authentic cadence,* or PAC as it's often called by acronym-loving music theorists, the two chords that make up the cadence are both in their root positions, meaning (as we discuss in Chapter 10) that the note on the bottom of the stack is the *root* (the note the chord is named after).

The strongest PAC occurs when the second chord, the I/i chord, has the root of the chord on both the bottom *and* the top of the stack of notes. This PAC makes for a high-impact end to a song.

Note in Figure 11-15 how the top note on the I chord is the same as the bottom note, making the root of the chord both the highest and lowest-pitched note of the chord.

Figure 11-15:
A perfect authentic cadence (PAC).

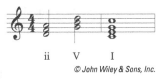

ii   V   I

© John Wiley & Sons, Inc.

Listen to Track 87 for an example of a perfect authentic cadence.

Imperfect authentic cadence

A V-I chord progression made with inverted chords — chords where the root, third, and fifth aren't in a perfect stack — is called an *imperfect authentic cadence* (IAC).

The difference between a PAC (see the preceding section) and an IAC is illustrated in Figure 11-16. Note how the PAC ends with the root of the chord in the root position, whereas the IAC ends with an inverted chord.

Figure 11-16:
Difference between a PAC and an IAC.

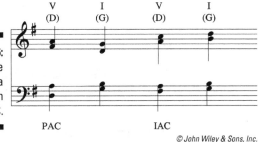

© John Wiley & Sons, Inc.

Listen to Track 88 to hear the difference between a perfect authentic cadence and an imperfect authentic cadence.

Plagal cadences

The harmonic goal of a *plagal cadence* is ultimately the four (IV/iv) chord, with the cadence occurring when that chord moves to the one (I/i) chord. Possible plagal cadences include IV-I, iv-i, iv-I, and IV-i.

This structure originated with medieval church music, mostly vocal music, and is therefore often referred to as the *Amen cadence.* If you're familiar with Gregorian chants or even many modern hymns, you've heard the Amen cadence in action. The cadence usually happens, not surprisingly, at the point where the chanters sing the two-chord "A-men."

"Amazing Grace," whose music is shown in Figure 11-17, contains a great example of a plagal cadence.

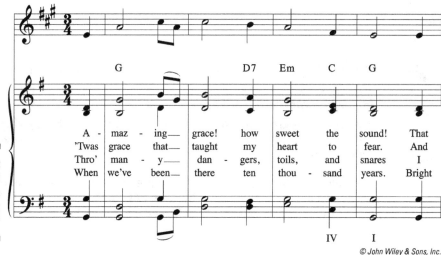

Figure 11-17: A plagal cadence in "Amazing Grace."

© John Wiley & Sons, Inc.

Listen to Track 89 to hear an example of a plagal cadence.

Plagal cadences are usually used within a song to end a phrase, instead of at the very end of a song, because they're not as decisive-sounding as perfect cadences are.

Figure 11-18 shows two more examples of plagal cadences.

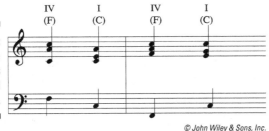

Figure 11-18:
Two more
examples
of plagal
cadences.

© John Wiley & Sons, Inc.

Listen to Track 90 to hear two more examples of plagal cadences.

Deceptive cadences

A *deceptive cadence* (sometimes called an *interrupted cadence*) reaches an ultimate point of tension on a V/v chord, just like the authentic cadence, but then it resolves to something other than the tonic (I/i) chord. Hence the name *deceptive cadence*. You think you're about to return to the I chord, but then you don't.

A deceptive cadence leads from the V/v chord to any chord *other* than the I/i chord. Deceptive cadences are considered one of the weakest cadences because they invoke a feeling of incompleteness.

The most common deceptive cadence, used 99 times out of 100, is when you have a V/v chord that moves up to a vi/VI chord. The phrase looks and feels like it's about to end and close with the I chord, but instead it moves up to the vi instead, as shown in Figure 11-19. The VI or vi is the most common second chord used in deceptive cadences because it shares two notes with the I chord and thus heightens the "deception" when a listener expects to hear I.

Figure 11-19:
Deceptive
cadence.

© John Wiley & Sons, Inc.

Listen to Track 91 to hear an example of a deceptive cadence.

Half-cadence

With a *half-cadence*, the musical phrase ends *at* the point of tension, the V/v chord itself. It basically plays to a V chord and stops, resulting in a musical phrase that feels unfinished. This cadence received its name because it just doesn't feel like it's done yet.

The most common form of half-cadence occurs when the V chord is preceded by the I chord in second inversion (when the fifth of a chord is the lowest-sounding note; see Chapter 10). This pattern produces two chords with the same bass note, as you can see in Figure 11-20. The first measure of the figure shows keyboard spacing, and the second measure shows vocal spacing.

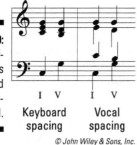

Figure 11-20: Half-cadences don't sound quite finished.

I   V   I   V
Keyboard   Vocal
spacing   spacing

© John Wiley & Sons, Inc.

Listen to Track 92 to hear an example of a half-cadence.

Part III
Musical Expression through Tempo and Dynamics

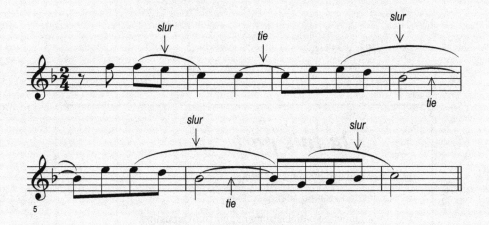

Visit www.dummies.com/extras/musictheory for an interesting article.

In this part . . .

- Read and use dynamic markings.
- Understand tempo changes.
- Get acquainted with instrument tone and acoustics.

Chapter 12

Creating Varied Sound through Tempo and Dynamics

In This Chapter

▷ Keeping time with tempo

▷ Controlling loudness with dynamics

▷ Access the audio tracks at www.dummies.com/go/musictheory

*E*verybody knows that making good music is about more than just stringing a collection of notes together. Music is just as much about communication as it is about making sounds. And in order to really communicate to your audience, you need to grab their attention, inspire them, and wring some sort of emotional response out of them.

Tempo (speed) and *dynamics* (volume) are two tools you can use to turn those carefully metered notes on sheet music into the elegant promenade of Liszt's Hungarian Rhapsody No. 2, the sweeping exuberance of Chopin's études, or, in a more modern context, the slow creepiness of Nick Cave's "Red Right Hand."

Tempo and dynamics are the markings in a musical sentence that tell you whether you're supposed to feel angry or happy or sad when you play a piece of music. These markings help a performer tell the composer's story to the audience. In this chapter, we help you get familiar with both concepts and their accompanying notation.

Taking the Tempo of Music

Tempo means "time," and when you hear people talk about the tempo of a musical piece, they're referring to the speed at which the music progresses. The point of tempo isn't necessarily how quickly or slowly you can play a musical piece, however. Tempo sets the basic mood of a piece of music. Music that's played very, very slowly, or *grave,* can impart a feeling of extreme somberness, whereas music played very, very quickly, or *prestissimo,* can seem maniacally happy and bright. (We explain these Italian terms, along with others, later in this section.)

The importance of tempo can truly be appreciated when you consider that the original purpose of much music was to accompany people dancing. Often the movement of the dancers' feet and body positions worked to set the tempo of the music, and the musicians followed the dancers.

Prior to the 17th century, composers had no real control over how their transcribed music would be performed by others, especially by those who had never heard the pieces performed by their creator. It was only in the 1600s that composers started using tempo (and dynamic) markings in sheet music. The following sections explain how tempo got its start and how it's used in music today.

Establishing a universal tempo: The minim

The first person to write a serious book about tempo and timing in music was the French philosopher and mathematician Marin Mersenne. From an early age, Mersenne was obsessed with the mathematics and rhythms that governed daily life — such as the heartbeats of mammals, the hoof beats of horses, and the wing flaps of various species of birds. This obsession led to his interest in the field of music theory, which was still in its infancy at the time.

With the 1636 release of his book, *Harmonie universelle,* Mersenne introduced the concept of a universal music tempo, called the *minim* (named after his religious order), which was equal to the beat of the human heart, around 70 to 75 beats per minute (bpm). Furthermore, Mersenne introduced the idea of splitting his minim into smaller units so that composers could begin adding more detail to their written music.

Mersenne's minim was greeted with open arms by the musical community. Since the introduction of written music a few hundred years before, composers had been trying to find some way to accurately reproduce the timing needed for other musicians to properly perform their written works. Musicians loved the concept because having a common beat unit to practice with made it easier for individual musicians to play the growing canon of musical standards with complete strangers.

Keeping steady time with a metronome

Despite what you may have gathered from horror movies such as Dario Argento's *Two Evil Eyes* and a number of Alfred Hitchcock's films, that pyramid-shaped ticking box does have a purpose besides turning human beings into mindless zombies.

Practicing with a metronome is the best possible way to learn how to keep a steady pace throughout a song, and it's one of the easiest ways to match the tempo of the piece you're playing to the tempo conceived by the person who wrote the piece.

The metronome was first invented in 1696 by the French musician and inventor Étienne Loulié. His first prototype consisted of a simple weighted pendulum and was called a *cronométre*. The problem with Loulié's invention, though, was that in order to work with beats as slow as 40 to 60 bpm, the device had to be at least 6 feet tall.

It wasn't until more than 100 years later that two German tinkerers, Dietrich Nikolaus Winkel and Johann Nepomuk Maelzel, worked independently to produce the spring-loaded design that's the basis for analog (non-electronic) metronomes today. Maelzel was the first to slap a patent on the finished product, and as a result, his initial is attached to the standard tempo sign, *MM = 120*. *MM* is short for *Maelzel's metronome,* and the *120* means that 120 bpm, or 120 quarter notes, should be played in the piece.

Like the concept of the minim (refer to the previous section), both musicians and composers warmly received the metronome. From then on, when composers wrote a piece of music, they could give musicians an exact number of beats per minute to be played. The metronomic markings were written over the staff so that musicians would know what to calibrate their metronomes to. For example, *quarter note = 96,* or *MM = 96,* means that 96 quarter notes should be played per minute in a given song. These markings are still used today for setting mostly electronic metronomes, particularly for classical and avant-garde compositions that require precise timing.

Translating tempo notation

Although the metronome was the perfect invention for control freaks like Beethoven, most composers were happy to instead use the growing vocabulary of tempo notation to generally describe the pace of a song. Even today, composers still use the same Italian words to describe tempo and pace in music. These words are in Italian simply because when these phrases came into use (1600–1750), the bulk of European music came from Italian composers.

Table 12-1 lists some of the most standard tempo notations in Western music, usually found written above the time signature at the beginning of a piece of music, as shown in Figure 12-1.

Table 12-1	Common Tempo Notation
Notation	*Description*
Grave	The slowest pace; very formal and very, very slow
Largo	Funeral march slow; very serious and somber
Larghetto	Slow, but not as slow as largo
Lento	Slow
Adagio	Leisurely; think graduation and wedding marches
Andante	Walking pace; close to the original minim
Andantino	Slightly faster than andante; think Patsy Cline's "Walking After Midnight," or any other lonely cowboy ballad you can think of
Moderato	Right smack in the middle; not fast or slow, just moderate
Allegretto	Moderately fast
Allegro	Quick, brisk, merry
Vivace	Lively, fast
Presto	Very fast
Prestissimo	Maniacally fast; think "Flight of the Bumblebee"

Figure 12-1:
Allegro
means the
music would
be played at
a brisk pace.

© John Wiley & Sons, Inc.

Just to make things a little more precise, modifying adverbs such as *molto* (very), *meno* (less), *poco* (a little), and *non troppo* (not too much) are sometimes used in conjunction with the tempo notation terms listed in Table 12-1. For example, if a piece of music says that the tempo is *poco allegro,* it means that the piece is to be played "a little fast," whereas *poco largo* would mean "a little slow."

If you have a metronome, try setting it to different speeds to get a feel of how different pieces of music may be played to each different setting.

Play Track 93 to hear examples of 80 (slow), 100 (moderate), and 120 (fast) beats per minute.

Speeding up and slowing down: Changing the tempo

Sometimes a different tempo is attached to a specific musical phrase within a song to set it apart from the rest. The following are a few tempo changes you're likely to encounter in written music:

- *Accelerando (accel.):* Gradually play faster and faster.
- *Stringendo:* Quickly play faster.
- *Doppio movimento:* Play phrase twice as fast.
- *Ritardando (rit., ritard., rallentando, or rall.):* Gradually play slower and slower.
- *Calando:* Play slower and softer.

At the end of musical phrases in which the tempo has been changed, you may see *a tempo,* which indicates a return to the original tempo of the piece.

Dealing with Dynamics: Loud and Soft

Dynamic markings tell you how loudly or softly to play a piece of music. Composers use dynamics to communicate how they want a piece of music to "feel" to an audience, whether it's quiet, loud, or aggressive, for example.

The most common dynamic markings, from softest to loudest, are shown in Table 12-2.

Table 12-2	Common Dynamic Notation	
Notation	**Abbreviation**	**Description**
Pianissimo	pp	Play very softly
Piano	p	Play softly
Mezzo piano	mp	Play moderately softly
Mezzo forte	mf	Play moderately loudly
Forte	f	Play loudly
Fortissimo	ff	Play very loudly

Dynamic markings can be placed at the beginning or anywhere else within a piece of music. For example, in the music shown in Figure 12-2, *pianissimo* *(pp)* means that the piece is to be played very softly until you reach the next dynamic marking. *Fortissimo (ff)* means that the rest of the selection is to be played very loudly.

Figure 12-2:
The dynamic markings here mean you would play the first bar very softly, *pia-nissimo,* and the second very loudly, *fortissimo.*

© John Wiley & Sons, Inc.

Modifying phrases

Sometimes when reading a piece of music, you may find one of the markings in Table 12-3 attached to a musical phrase or a section of music generally four to eight measures long.

Table 12-3	Common Modifying Phrases	
Notation	*Abbreviation*	*Description*
Crescendo	*cresc.*	Play gradually louder
Diminuendo	*dim.*	Play gradually softer

In Figure 12-3, the long *cresc.*, called a *hairpin*, means to play the selection gradually louder and louder until you reach the end of the *crescendo.*

Figure 12-3:
The *crescendo* here means play gradually louder and louder until the end of the hairpin.

© John Wiley & Sons, Inc.

In Figure 12-4, the hairpin beneath the phrase means to play the selection gradually softer and softer until you reach the end of the *diminuendo.*

Figure 12-4:
The *diminuendo,* or *decrescendo,* here means play gradually softer and softer until the end of the hairpin.

© John Wiley & Sons, Inc.

Another common marking you'll probably come across in written music is a *slur,* which you can see in Figure 12-5. Just like when your speech is slurred and the words stick together, a musical slur is to be played with all the notes "slurring" into one another. Slurs look like curves that connect the notes.

Figure 12-5:
Slurs over
groups of
notes.

© John Wiley & Sons, Inc.

Checking out other dynamic markings

You probably won't see any of the following notations in a beginning-to-intermediate piece of music, but for more advanced pieces, you may find one or two (listed alphabetically):

- *Agitato:* Excitedly, agitated
- *Animato:* With spirit
- *Appassionato:* Impassioned
- *Con forza:* Forcefully, with strength
- *Dolce:* Sweetly
- *Dolente:* Sadly, with great sorrow
- *Grandioso:* Grandly
- *Legato:* Smoothly, with the notes flowing from one to the next
- *Sotto voce:* Barely audible

The piano: A composer's universal tool

Since its creation, the piano has been the universal tool of choice for composing music, because almost every note you would ever want to work with is present right there in front of you on the keyboard. Most pianos have at least seven octaves to work with, and a few concert pianos have eight.

You want to compose music for a bassoon? The lower registers of the piano work quite nicely. Pieces written for strings can be easily hammered out in the middle and upper registers. And unlike most other instruments, you can play chords and multiple notes simultaneously on a piano, which works well for trying to figure out how that multi-instrument orchestral piece you're writing will eventually sound.

You can blame the fact that the piano was invented by an Italian, Bartolomeo Cristofori, for the bulk of tempo and dynamic markings being Italian words. From the first day of the piano's release to the initially Italian market, composers were finding new ways to write music on this spectacularly flexible instrument.

Examining the piano pedal dynamics

Additional dynamic markings relate to the use of the three foot pedals located at the base of the piano (some pianos have only two pedals). The standard modern piano pedal setup is, from left to right:

- **Soft pedal (or *una corda* pedal):** On most modern upright pianos, the soft pedal moves the resting hammers inside the piano closer to their corresponding strings. Because the hammers have less distance to travel to reach the string, the speed at which they hit the strings is reduced, and the volume of the resulting notes is therefore much quieter and has less sustain.

  Most modern grand pianos have three strings per note, so when you press a key, the hammer strikes all three simultaneously. The soft pedal is called *una corda* ("one string") because it moves all the hammers to the right so that they only strike one of the strings. This effectively cuts the volume of the sound by two-thirds.

- **Middle pedal:** If it's present (many modern pianos have only the two outer pedals to work with), the middle pedal has a variety of roles, depending on the piano. On some American pianos, this pedal gives the notes a tinny, honky-tonk piano sound when depressed. Some other pianos have a bass sustain pedal as their middle pedal. It works like a sustain pedal but only for the bass half of the piano keyboard.

Still other pianos — specifically many concert pianos — have a *sostenuto* pedal for their middle pedal, which works to sustain one or more notes indefinitely, while allowing successive notes to be played without sustain.

✔ **Damper pedal (or sustaining or loud pedal):** The damper pedal does exactly the opposite of what the name would imply — when this pedal is pressed, the damper inside the piano *lifts off* the strings and allows the notes being played to die out naturally. This creates a ringing, echoey effect for single notes and chords (which can be heard, for example, at the very end of The Beatles's "A Day in the Life"). The damper pedal can also make for a really muddled sound if too much of a musical phrase is played with the pedal held down.

In sheet music notation, the entire musical phrase to be altered by use of pedals is horizontally bracketed, with the name of the pedal to be used listed beside or beneath it. If no pedal number is given, the damper pedal is to be automatically used for the selection.

For example, in Figure 12-6, the "Ped." signifies that the damper pedal (usually the foot pedal farthest to your right) is to be depressed during the selection. The breaks in the brackets (shown with ∧) mean that in these places, you briefly lift your foot off the pedal.

Figure 12-6:
Pedal dynamics show you which pedal to use and how long to hold it down.

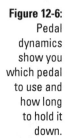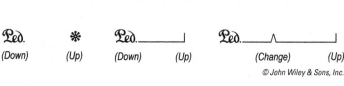

Ped.   ✳   *Ped.*＿＿＿」   *Ped.*＿＿∧＿＿＿」
(Down)   (Up)   (Down)   (Up)   (Change)   (Up)

© John Wiley & Sons, Inc.

Looking at the articulation markings for other instruments

Although most articulation markings are considered universal instructions — that is, applicable to all instruments — some are aimed specifically at certain musical instruments. Table 12-4 lists some of these markings and their respective instruments.

Table 12-4	Articulation Markings for Specific Instruments
Notation	*What It Means*
Stringed instruments	
Martellato	A short, hammered stroke played with very short bow strokes
Pizzicato	To pluck the string or strings with your fingers
Spiccato	With a light, bouncing motion of the bow
Tremolo	Quickly playing the same sequence of notes on a stringed instrument
Vibrato	Slight change of pitch on the same note, producing a vibrating, trembling sound
Horns	
Chiuso	With the horn bell stopped up (to produce a flatter, muted effect)
Vocals	
A capella	Without any musical accompaniment
Choro	The chorus of the song
Parlando or parlante	Singing in a speaking, oratory style
Tessitura	The average range used in a piece of vocal music

From harpsichord to piano

The concept of using dynamic markings in sheet music came about around the same time as the piano — and for good reason. Before the invention of the piano by Bartolomeo Cristofori in 1709, most composers were confined to writing most of their pieces for the harpsichord, an instrument without the capability to play both soft and loud sounds easily.

Here's why varying the sounds is difficult: The basic internal design of the harpsichord follows the design of a stringed instrument. However, instead of having one's fingers in direct contact with the string (as with a guitar or fiddle), harpsichords are fitted with a plucking mechanism inside the instrument itself. When a certain key is pressed, the corresponding internal string is plucked by the mechanism. No matter how hard or soft you press the instrument's keys, the resulting volume is pretty much the same.

Although the piano looks a lot like a harpsichord, it's really very different. The piano incorporates a hammer-and-lever mechanism that strikes each string with the same force as the human finger on the piano key did; the fact that a hammer hits a string every time you press a key is why the piano is considered a percussive instrument. The piano made both quiet and loud sounds possible on the same instrument, and, therefore, in the same musical piece. This flexibility is why the piano was originally named the *gravicembalo col pian e forte*, or "harpsichord with soft and loud." The name was later shortened to pianoforte and, finally, to simply piano.

Chapter 13

Instrument Tone Color and Acoustics

*H*ave you ever wondered why more songs don't use a tuba or a bassoon for the lead instrument, or why so many great parts for instruments have been taken by pianos and guitars? Okay, maybe you haven't thought that much about it, but if you're considering writing music, you probably should.

The simple explanation for why some instruments are used for lead lines in music and others aren't is that the human ear reacts more favorably to higher-pitched sounds than to lower-pitched ones. Notice that it is the higher-pitched range that babies and small children babble in, that birds sing in, and that pretty much all the happy little things make noise in. People can't get away from enjoying these sounds — it's part of the human wiring.

High-pitched notes also convey a greater sense of immediacy. You can bow the cello until your arm falls off, but it's not going to sound as urgent and lively as it would if the same passage were played at the same speed on a violin. Similarly, when you're trying to get an idea across in conversation, especially an important idea, your voice tone tends to drift up toward the higher registers, not down into the lower ones. This is why lead instruments are sometimes called *talking* instruments.

In this chapter, we examine what constitutes instrument tone and what makes each instrument sound just the way it does. We also discuss basic acoustics and instrument harmonics, and explain why small ensembles and orchestras are put together the way they are.

Delving into Tone Color

The *tone color,* or character, of an instrument is made up of three basic components:

- ✔ Attack
- ✔ Timbre (or harmonic content)
- ✔ Decay

These three factors are what make every instrument sound different. Even if you're hearing the instrument through your car radio speakers, you can immediately tell, just by listening, what instrument is being played. We discuss each of these factors in the following sections.

Attack: Checking out the beginning sound of a note

The *attack* is the very first sound you notice when you hear a note, and it's possibly the most distinguishing aspect of a note played by an instrument. The violin, piano, and guitar all have their own distinctive attacks. Here's a brief rundown of each:

- ✔ **Violin:** When you hear the first microsecond of a violin being played, you instantly know it's a violin because of that quick, raw sound of a bow being drawn across the familiar-sounding string. It's beautiful, immediate, and unmistakable. You don't even know you're hearing the first tiny point of contact, but it's there. If you were to slow down a recording of any virtuoso's violin solo, you would find that gorgeous, familiar rasp at the beginning of every bow stroke.

- ✔ **Piano:** Each time you hit the key of a piano, a tiny hammer strikes three metal strings simultaneously, producing a beautiful, ringing attack. It's even more amazing to open up a piano and listen to how each note sounds when the frontpiece or lid isn't muffling the sound.

- ✔ **Guitar:** The guitar's distinctive attack is a sharp little twang when the metal strings are first plucked. However, the sound is definitely less pronounced when the guitar has nylon strings. The different types of strings are partly responsible for the variety of guitar-playing styles by musicians. Rock, pop, and country songs are usually played with metal-strung guitars because the metal strings provide a nice, crisp, aggressive-sounding twang. Classical, flamenco, and much of folk music use nylon-strung guitars because the attack is much softer-sounding, making for mellower music.

The speed of an instrument's attack can play just as big a role in the sound of an instrument: The plucking of a string on a harpsichord is quick and sharp, which is much different from the languorous drawing of a bow across the strings of a double bass.

Timbre: Hearing the body of a note

The *timbre* (pronounced *tam*-ber), or harmonic content, of an instrument is what determines the middle part, or body, of each played note. When you remove the attack and the decay of some instruments' sounds with digital equipment, you find a lot of surprising similarities between instruments. (You can read about decay in the next section.)

For example, the timbre and pitch range of a flute and violin are almost identical, but because one is blown and one is bowed, the initial attack of each separate note is completely different and identifies these instruments by their very first split-second sounds.

However, the *harmonics* — or sound waves — between some instruments are radically different, simply because of their construction. For example, the harmonic content between a note on a guitar and the same note on a piano is completely different, because one note on a guitar is one string being plucked, but one note on a piano is actually three strings being hit with a hammer.

Any sound, no matter the source, is caused by something vibrating. Without vibration, sound doesn't exist. These vibrations cause the air particles next to the source to vibrate as well, and those air particles, in turn, cause the particles next to them to vibrate, and so on and so on, creating a sound wave. Just like a wave in water, the farther out the sound wave moves, the weaker it gets, until it completely dissipates. If the original vibration creates a strong enough wave, though, it eventually reaches your ears and registers as a sound.

You hear sounds because air vibrates against your eardrums, causing them to vibrate. These vibrations are then analyzed by your brain and registered as music, traffic, birds singing — whatever. Because sound waves are picked up by each unique eardrum and dissected by each unique brain, chances are that nobody hears the same sound exactly the same as anybody else.

Each complete vibration of a sound wave is called a *cycle*. The number of cycles completed in one second is called the *frequency* of the vibration. One of the most noticeable differences between two sounds is the difference in pitch; the frequency of a sound determines its pitch. Frequency is measured in *hertz*, with one hertz (Hz) being one cycle per second. One thousand hertz is called a *kilohertz* and is written as 1 kHz. A high-frequency vibration produces a high-pitched note; a low-frequency vibration gives a low-pitched note.

The human hearing range (audible range) is about 16 Hz to 16 kHz. The frequencies of notes that can be played on a piano range from 27.5 Hz to just over 4 kHz.

Instruments get their specific sounds because their sounds come from many different tones all sounding together at different frequencies. A single note played on a piano, for example, actually consists of several tones all sounding together at slightly different frequencies, or multiples of the frequency base. The musical note produced by a tuning fork is called a *pure tone* because it consists of one tone sounding at just one frequency.

Reproducing "natural" sounds with synthesizers

When the first synthesizers were developed, the designers were attempting to reproduce "natural" instruments instead of just synthetic sounds (like the flat, artificial sound of a 1970s synthesizer, for example). The developers of the synthesizer discovered that the biggest challenge in making it sound natural wasn't in reproducing another instrument's timbre — which is what the engineers had primarily focused on from the onset — but in reproducing the attack and decay of each instrument. Eventually, they had to record samples of the instruments themselves into the synthesizers in order to make sounds distinguishable from one another.

Decay: Listening for the final sound of a note

Decay is the final part of an instrument's played note. Here are the two types of instrument decay:

- **Impulsive:** An *impulsive* decay belongs to instruments that need to be played continuously, or in pulses, in order to continue sounding. Tones are produced and immediately begin to decay until the next note played starts the process again. Common examples of instruments with an impulsive decay are those produced by plucking or striking, such as the guitar, most percussion instruments, and the piano.

- **Sustained:** A *sustained* decay is one for which the vibrating column of an instrument, such as the body of a flute, clarinet, or other column-shaped instrument, is excited continuously so that the sound continues in a more or less steady state as long as the note is being played. Instruments producing sustained tones are those that are bowed or blown, such as violins and other bowed stringed instruments, woodwinds, free-reed instruments such as the accordion, and brass instruments.

Building the Band: An Acoustics Lesson

Next time you go out to see an orchestra or a big band play, or even when you watch one of those late-night show bands perform on TV, take a look at where the performers are sitting in relation to each other. Pay particular attention to which instrument is the "lead" instrument.

As you study an orchestra or band, you'll likely notice these two things:

- **Especially in an orchestral setting, all the performers playing the same instruments are sitting together.** This setup isn't because they all have to share the same piece of sheet music — it's because when you stick two violins or flutes or clarinets together they sound louder and fuller. If you stick *ten* of them together, you've got a wall of sound coming at you from that area of the orchestra.

  Incidentally, this setup is one reason instruments are so challenging to play. They're not particularly tricky to play well in themselves, but you often have to play them in exact synchronization with other performers.

✔ **The lead instruments are in front of all the other instruments, especially in acoustic performances.** This setup is beneficial because of volume and perception: The sound waves from the instruments in the front of the ensemble will be heard a microsecond before the rest of the band and will, therefore, be perceived as being louder because you hear them a split second before the other instruments.

This principle applies to a regular four-piece electric band setting, too. If you want your singer to be heard above the guitars, make sure the amplifier carrying his or her voice is placed closer to the audience than the guitar and bass amp.

The best place to sit at an orchestral performance is directly behind the conductor but far enough back to be at the same height level as him. Conductors build each orchestra for each performance around where they stand so they can hear exactly what's being played. Similarly, this situation makes it pretty easy for a seasoned audio engineer to record an orchestral performance. Put the microphones right where the conductor's standing, and you'll record the piece of music exactly as the conductor intended for it to be heard.

Part IV
Musical Expression through Form

Visit www.dummies.com/extras/musictheory for an interesting article.

In this part . . .

✔ Discover the structure of different kinds of music.

✔ Explore different forms and genres of music.

Chapter 14

The Building Blocks of Music: Rhythm, Melody, Harmony, and Song Form

In This Chapter

▶ Reviewing rhythm, melody, and harmony

▶ Understanding musical phrases and periods

▶ Picking out and labeling the parts of a song

*W*hen we talk about musical *form,* we mean the structural blueprint used to create a specific type of music. For example, if you want to write a sonata, you follow a specific song structure. Although style elements like the basic melody, theme, and key signature would be entirely up to you, the way the sonata as a whole fits together — the beginning, middle, and ending — is set right from the beginning by the constraints of the sonata form itself.

In many ways, knowing how form works makes composing music extremely easy. After all, the pattern's already there — you just have to fill in the blanks. The real challenge is making your particular sonata, fugue, or concerto stand out from every other piece of music written in that form.

A lot of crossover exists between the definitions of form and genre, but they are two different concepts. *Genre* is more about how music sounds, regardless of its structure; examples are jazz, pop, country, and classical (although there are also certain forms unique to classical music).

The problem with identifying forms in modern music is that new music is still evolving. Students of music form in the 21st century may soon be studying anti-4/4 math-rock pioneers like Steve Albini alongside the composers Philip Glass and Beethoven.

In this chapter, we explain exactly what we mean when we refer to "musical form," and we discuss some of the more common musical forms you can encounter.

Establishing Rhythm

We can't talk about form and genre without talking about rhythm, which is the most basic element of music. You can write a piece of music without a melody line or without harmonic accompaniment, but you just can't write a piece of music without rhythm — unless, of course, your "music" is one single, sustained note with no variations in pitch.

Often, the rhythm differentiates one genre from another — such as the difference between alternative rock and punk rock, for example. Put a faster tempo to any Son Volt or Wilco song, and you can file the result in the same section of the record store as the Ramones and the Sex Pistols. Change the inherent rhythm patterns of a song, even a Sex Pistols song, and you can change it to anything from a tango to a waltz. Rhythm is *that* important to genre.

Rhythm moves through music as a generative force in several different ways. It creates the basic pulse of a song, as discussed in Part I of this book. Rhythm is the part of the song your toes tap along to and your head nods to. Meter helps organize notes into groups using a time signature and defines the repetitive pattern of strong and weak beats that noticeably move a song along. (The individual measures in a piece of music determine the meter; see Chapter 4 for more about measures.) This pulse creates a feeling of familiarity and expectation for the listener so that, theoretically, you can throw a pile of unexpected, jangly notes and chords at the listener and still retain a feeling of connection with your audience by holding on to them with the same, steady beat.

The actual rhythm that you hear when you listen to a song is usually referred to as the *surface rhythm.* For example, often when people say they like the *beat* of a pop song, they mean they enjoy the surface rhythm, which may simply be a rhythmic pattern on the drums. Sometimes the surface rhythm matches the underlying pulse of a song (the beat as determined by the time signature that governs the entire piece of music), especially in pop music, where the drums and the bass lines usually follow the basic beat. But sometimes, because of *syncopation* (which emphasizes the "off" beats), the surface rhythm and the pulse don't match up.

Tempo comes into play when you discuss the speed of the rhythm of a piece. Is it going to move along quickly and lively or somberly and slowly?

The speed at which a piece of music is played determines the overall feeling of the music for the audience. Rarely do you have a super-happy song played slowly and quietly, nor do you hear a super-sad song played at "Flight of the Bumblebee" speeds (see Chapter 12 for more about tempo).

Shaping the Melody

Most often, the melody is the part of the song you can't get out of your head. The *melody* is the lead line of a song — the part that the harmony is built around, and the part that gives as much glimpse into the emotion of a piece as the rhythm does. (Refer to the later section on harmony for more information.)

Much of melody's expressive power comes from the upward or downward flow of pitch. The pitch of a song goes up, and it can make the song sound like it's getting either more tense or more lively; the pitch of a song goes down, and it can give that part of the song an increased melancholic or dark feel. The shape of the pitch's travels is called its *contour*.

Here are the four common *melodic contours:*

- Arch
- Wave
- Inverted arch
- Pivotal

Contour simply means that the melody is shaped a certain way; the shape of a melody is especially easy to pick out when you have the sheet music right in front of you. The possibilities for building melodic phrases with just four basic contours are virtually infinite. (By *building melodic phrases,* we mean starting at the I chord, going up to the IV or V chord, and ending at the I chord; see Chapter 11 for more information about chord progressions.) For more information about composing music, *Music Composition For Dummies* by Scott Jarrett and Holly Day (Wiley) is a good place to start.

Figure 14-1 shows a stretch of music that has an *arch contour*. Note how the melody line in the treble clef first goes up in pitch from a low point to a high point and how it then goes back down again, creating the arch. When music goes up in pitch gradually like this, it results in an increase in tension in that section of the composition. The lower the pitch gets in such a gradual arch, the more the level of tension decreases.

Figure 14-1: In the arch contour, the pitch of notes goes up and then down.

Figure 14-2 shows music with a *wave contour*. Note how the melody line goes up, and down, and up again, and down again — just like a series of waves.

Figure 14-2: In the wave contour, pitch goes up and down and up and down, like waves on the sea.

Figure 14-3 shows music with an *inverted arch contour.* You may have noticed that the music in Figure 14-3 looks a lot like that in Figure 14-1. The only difference is that the melody line in Figure 14-3 goes down in pitch and then up to the end of the phrase. Therefore, the phrase starts out sounding relaxed and calm but contains an increase in tension as the arch rises toward the end of the phrase.

Figure 14-3: In the inverted arch contour, the pitch starts out high, goes down, and then heads up again.

Figure 14-4 shows an example of music with a *pivotal contour.* A pivotal melody line essentially pivots around the central note of the piece — in the case of the music in Figure 14-4, the E. A pivotal contour is a lot like a wave contour, except that the movement above and below the central note is minimal and continuously returns to that central note. Traditional folk music uses this melodic pattern a lot.

Figure 14-4:
The pivotal contour revolves around a certain pitch.

© John Wiley & Sons, Inc.

Any melody line in a piece of music generally falls into one of the preceding categories of contour. Try randomly picking up a piece of sheet music and tracing out the melody pattern yourself to see what we mean.

The *range* of a melody is determined by the interval between the highest and lowest pitches of the song. The rise and fall of tension is often proportional to its range. Melodies with a narrow pitch range tend to have only a slight amount of musical tension in them, whereas melodies with a wide range of pitches are more likely to have a greater level of tension. As the range of pitches in a song is widened, the potential for greater levels of tension increases.

Complementing the Melody with Harmony

Harmony is the part of the song that fills out the musical ideas expressed in the melody (see the preceding section for more on melody). Often, when you build a harmony based on a melodic line, you're essentially filling in the missing notes of the chord progressions used in the song. For example, take a look at the simple melody line shown in Figure 14-5.

Figure 14-5: A simple melody line in the key of C.

You can fill out the harmony in Figure 14-5 by simply grabbing the notes of the I and V chords and placing them in the bass line, as shown in Figure 14-6.

Figure 14-6: Harmony for a melody line in the key of C.

To put it really simply, harmony is all about the building of *chords,* which are tones coming from the scale in which the music is composed. (You can read more about chords in Chapter 10.) Harmony also stems from the order of the chord progressions themselves, and also how a phrase resolves itself through the V-I or IV-I cadence (see Chapter 11 for coverage of cadences).

Consonant harmonies are those that sound stable and pleasing to the ear, such as the I chord at the end of a phrase. *Dissonant* harmonies sound unstable and unpleasant to the ear; they may sound wrong or seem to clash until they're resolved into consonant harmonies. Tension can be created in a song through harmony by creating dissonance, often by adding extra third intervals on top of a triad to build sevenths, ninths, and so on. (Check out Chapter 9 for coverage of intervals.) Many seventh chords are dissonant harmonies. Composers also use the tension between consonance and dissonance to establish a sense of a beginning and ending in a song.

Working with Musical Phrases and Periods

Two of the building blocks of musical form are phrases and periods. A *musical phrase* is the smallest unit of music with a defined beginning and end. Most musical phrases consist of a beginning I chord progressing to a IV or a V chord and ending again on the I chord. Theoretically, thousands of chord progressions may exist between that first I chord and the IV or V chord. However, you may lose your audience in that time.

Musical phrases are like sentences in a paragraph — just as most readers don't want to wade through a thousand lines of text to find out the point of a sentence, most music audiences are listening for the musical idea expressed in a phrase and get bored if it sounds like you're just meandering between chords and not coming to a resolution.

So how long should a musical phrase be? It's really up to the composer, but generally, a phrase is usually two to four measures long. Within that space, a phrase begins, works through one or more chord progressions, and resolves itself back to the I chord. (Check out Chapter 11 for the scoop on chord progressions.)

When a composer really wants you to understand that a group of measures are to be linked together in a phrase and played as an important unit — kind of like a topic sentence in an essay — he or she links the phrase together with a curved line called a *phrase line,* as shown in Figure 14-7. Notice how the phrase both begins and ends on the I chord, or the G major chord. (The numbers above the Roman numerals are fingering markings for the pianist; you don't need to worry about them.)

Figure 14-7: Note the phrase line in the bass clef.

© John Wiley & Sons, Inc.

Don't confuse phrase lines with ties and slurs. A phrase line ties an entire musical phrase together, whereas slurs and ties only tie together a small part of a phrase. (If you want to read about ties, head to Chapter 2. We discuss slurs in Chapter 12.)

The phrase represents the smallest unit ending with a cadence in a piece of music. The next larger unit used in musical form is the period. Musical *periods* are created when two or three musical phrases are linked together. In the case of musical periods, the first musical phrase is one that ends in a half-cadence (ending *at* the V/v chord), and the second phrase ends with an authentic cadence (ending with the V/v chord resolving to the I/i chord). We cover cadences in Chapter 11.

The half-cadence comes across like a comma in a sentence, with the authentic cadence, or consequent, ending the linked phrases like a period.

Figure 14-8 shows an example of a musical period.

Figure 14-8:
A musical period is made of linked phrases.

© John Wiley & Sons, Inc.

Linking Musical Parts to Create Forms

The division of music into *parts* occurs when you link two or more periods that sound like they belong together. (See the preceding section for a discussion of periods.) They share major harmonic focal points, similar melody lines, and similar rhythm structure. They may have other resemblances, too. Parts can be further linked together to create musical *forms.*

Composers conventionally give alphabetic labels to the musical parts within a composition: A, B, C, and so forth. If a part is repeated in a song, its letter also is repeated. For example, ABA is a familiar layout in classical music, where the opening *theme,* or the main musical idea that runs through a song (labeled A), after vanishing during part B, is repeated at the end of the song.

As the *contrast form,* where you have different musical sections that can differ widely from one another, AB forms come in a boundless array of possibilities. You may see recurring sections, unique ones, or any combination of both. For example, a *rondo* — a popular form in classical music — alternates between a recurring section and others that occur one time each. A rondo, then, would be labeled ABACADA . . . (and so on).

You may even encounter an *ongoing form,* which has no recurrence whatsoever: ABCDE. . . . This form creates what's known as a *through-composed* piece of music.

In the following sections, we describe some of the most common forms you may encounter in music.

Rachel Grimes, composer, on the limits of form

"In school, there's the tendency to get didactic about theory, so you get into this mind-set that only certain chord progressions are allowed, and all the rest aren't. Pop music is very didactic that way. There are certain expected standards, like you're not allowed to go to a VI chord after resolving to a IV or a V — you're just expected to go to the I, and there really isn't much deviation from that pattern. I think the biggest challenge for students and users of music theory is to accept that certain groundwork has been laid out for them, so far as what sounds 'right' in Western music, but that deviations from that groundwork and those patterns are still allowed".

One-part form (A)

The *one-part form*, also known as *A form* or *unbroken form*, is the most primitive song structure and is also sometimes referred to as the *air form* or *ballad form*. In a one-part form, a simple melody is repeated with slight changes to accommodate different words, as in a *strophic* song like "Old McDonald Had a Farm." This song repeats the same musical line but changes the words with each verse.

The one-part form is mostly found in folk songs, carols, or other songs that are short and have a limited theme and movement. A forms come only in a single variety. They may be long or short, but they're always described as A (or AA, or even AAA).

Binary form (AB)

Binary form consists of two contrasting sections that function as statement counterstatement. The pattern may be a simple AB, as in "My Country, 'Tis of Thee," or in simple minuets, where the form is usually AABB, with the second A and second B being variations of the first A and B.

In the binary form used in the Baroque period, the pattern can involve a change of key, usually to the key of the fifth of the original key if the piece is in a major key. Part A begins in one key and ends in the key of the fifth, while part B begins in the new key and ends in the original key. Each part is repeated, giving the pattern AABB.

Musicians reflect on knowing when a song is done

Steve Reich (composer): "When I start out, I always have a rough idea of how much time I have to work with a piece of music, whether it's going to be a long piece or a short piece of music. And that's often dependent on whoever's commissioning the piece. Exactly how long it is, how many minutes it ends up being — that's worked out by musical intuition, which is the rock-bottom foundation of composing music for me, and, I think, for most composers. In other words, you sketch out the number of movements you're going to have, and the basic harmonies you're going to be using to get through the movements, and the rest is worked out in detail largely by intuition, by listening to the music itself."

Barry Adamson (Nick Cave and the Bad Seeds): "I guess there's a point where all the criteria are satisfied, and also, sometimes there's an immediate feeling that you didn't write the song, that it's something perfect and separate from yourself, because now you're hearing the finished thing and you can't remember how it was put together."

Momus (a.k.a. Nick Currie): "I work very quickly. Concept, lyrical notes, chord structure, bass line, percussion, more arrangement, vocal, mix. It's usually all done in one ultra-concentrated session of perhaps eight hours. A day's work. It's finished when you get the mix you like, simple as that. It's important to me not to leave things open. I like to make quick decisions, and bring things to a conclusion. This is probably one reason I'm so prolific."

John Hughes III (soundtrack composer): "With me? I don't know. I think that's the biggest problem for me. I know, with other musicians, too, it's just sort of not knowing when to stop. So, usually, I usually feel my best stuff is the stuff I don't feel like I have to keep working on. Usually, if there's something that I keep on adding stuff to, and changing it over and over, it's probably already dead, and the core of it just isn't right. Usually, my favorite stuff, I'll get done really quick, and the longer I dwell on it — I don't know if it's just because I get sick of it or what — but you just kind of know when something's done."

Mika Vainio (Pan Sonic): "When we feel that the song is bearable."

Three-part form (ABA)

Songs frequently take the form ABA, known as *three-part form* or *ternary/ tertiary form*. This simple form is produced by varying and repeating the melody. For example, "Twinkle, Twinkle, Little Star" states a tune, varies it, and then restates it (which makes it ABA form). The B part here may be called the *bridge,* or the link, between the two A parts.

Here's how the three-part song form works:

- ✔ The first part, A, may be played once or repeated immediately.
- ✔ The middle part, B, is a contrasting section, meaning it's different than the first section.
- ✔ The last part is the same or very similar to the first part, A.

Three-part ABA form extends the idea of statement and departure by bringing back the first section. Both contrast and repetition are used in this form. Pop music is frequently a variation on ABA, called AABA, while blues is often AAB. AABA form is used in songs like "Over the Rainbow."

Arch form (ABCBA)

Music written in *arch form* is made up of three parts: A, B, and C. In arch form, the A, B, and C are played sequentially, and then part B is played a second time, directly following the C, and the song ends with the replaying of the A part.

Composer Béle Bartók used this form in many of his pieces, including his Piano Concerto No. 2 and Violin Concerto No. 2. More recent examples include Steve Reich's "The Desert Music" and Hella's "Biblical Violence."

Chapter 15

Relying on Classical Forms

In This Chapter
▷ Understanding counterpoint and how it began
▷ Reviewing the many classical and enduring forms

During the Golden Age of classical music, from the late 1700s to the mid-1800s, composers were competing viciously with one another to create new and more vibrant types of music. With the adoption of the piano by classical artists, existing ways of playing music could be further developed, including counterpoint, which uses both hands to create melody and harmony. In this chapter, we explain the development of counterpoint and its use in a variety of classical forms and genres, from sonatas and rondos to fugues, symphonies, and more.

Counterpoint as a Classical Revelation

The most famous development in the Golden Age of classical music was the emergence of counterpoint as a popular musical technique. Composers of the period began writing music for the left hand that was just as complicated as the music written for the right. The left-hand music they created often mirrored closely what the right hand had been playing.

Prior to the Classical period, the bass line in most music was limited to simple melodic accompaniment. This limited use of the bass line was a carryover from the music of the Catholic Church, where the organ provided simple bass lines (figured bass) to accompany vocalists.

The invention of counterpoint not only enhanced the melody of musical arrangements, but it also blurred exactly where the melody ended and the harmony began. Almost every classical composer, using all the forms discussed in this chapter, has used counterpoint in his or her own music — even the right-handed ones. Figure 15-1 shows an example of counterpoint.

Figure 15-1:
Example
of counter
point from
J.S. Bach's
"Aus
meines
Herzens
Grunde"
("From the
Depths of
My Heart").

© John Wiley & Sons, Inc.

Sussing Out the Sonata

The *sonata* was the most popular form used by instrumental composers from the mid-18th century until the beginning of the 20th century. This form is considered by many to be the first true break from the liturgical music that had made such an impact on Western music from the Medieval period on through the Baroque period.

Sonatas are based on the song (ternary) form, ABA, which means they have three defined parts: exposition, development, and recapitulation. (For more on the song form and other common forms, check out Chapter 14.) The true genius of the sonata is that not only does its structure allow many of the rules of basic music theory to be broken, but it also *encourages* such defiance. With a sonata, it's perfectly allowable to switch to a new key and time signature in the middle of the song. In the following sections, we explain the three parts of a sonata.

Starting with the exposition

The first part of a sonata, called the *exposition,* presents the basic thematic material of the *movement,* or each self-contained part of a piece of music. This part is also often broken up into two thematic parts:

- ✔ **First part:** Generally, the first part of the exposition presents the main theme of the song, or the musical "thread" that ties the piece together. This first part usually is the line that sticks the most in your head.

- ✔ **Second part:** The second part of the exposition is a "reflection" of the first part, in that it sounds a lot like the first part but is slightly changed.

Put on Beethoven's Sonata in C Minor, Opus 13 to get a good example of these two defined parts, or look at the excerpts shown in Figures 15-2 and 15-3 from the same sonata.

Figure 15-2:
Excerpt from the opening theme, first part, of Beethoven's Sonata in C Minor, Opus 13.

© John Wiley & Sons, Inc.

Figure 15-3:
Excerpt from the second part of Sonata in C Minor, Opus 13, which is a reflective theme of the first.

© John Wiley & Sons, Inc.

Moving on to something new: Development

The second part of the sonata form, called the *development,* often sounds like it belongs to a completely different piece of music altogether. In this part, you can move through different key signatures and explore musical ideas that are completely different from the original theme.

Often this part of the sonata is the most exciting. Here you can include your big chords and increase tension with the use of stronger rhythm and greater *interval content* (number of interval steps between each note).

Figure 15-4 shows an excerpt from the development of Sonata in C Minor, Opus 13.

Figure 15-4: Excerpt from the second part, or development, of Beethoven's Sonata in C Minor, Opus 13.

© John Wiley & Sons, Inc.

Taking a rest with recapitulation

After the excitement of a sonata's development, it feels natural to come to rest where you began. The third and final part of a sonata is the *recapitulation,* where the composition returns to the original key and the musical theme expressed in the first section and brings it all to a close. Figure 15-5 shows an excerpt of the final movement of Beethoven's Sonata No. 8. Sonata in C Minor, Opus 13.

Figure 15-5:
Excerpt
from the
third part of
Beethoven's
Sonata
No. 8.
Sonata in
C Minor,
Opus 13.

© John Wiley & Sons, Inc.

Rounding Up the Rondo

Rondos expand on the freedom of expression inherent in the sonata form (see the earlier section "Sussing Out the Sonata") by allowing even more disparate sections of music to be joined together by a common musical section. The formula for a rondo is ABACA.... Technically, with a rondo you can indefinitely continue adding brand new sections — featuring different keys or time signatures — to a particular piece so long as you keep linking them together with the opening (A) theme. The A section of Mozart's *Rondo Alla Turca* ties more than six different musical ideas together using this form. See Figure 15-6 for an excerpt.

Figure 15-6:
Excerpt from the A section of Mozart's *Rondo Alla Turca.*

Figuring Out the Fugue

Another major musical form to come out of the Classical period was the *fugue,* the form fully developed by Bach, although it had been around for a century or so prior. A fugue is a highly evolved form of imitative counter-point, in which two (or more) musical lines use the same theme, either at the same pitch or transposed. Fugues are defined by the way the notes in the treble clef and the notes in the bass clef switch off carrying the main theme and driving the rhythm of the piece, resulting in a call-and-response feel.

Note, for example, in Figure 15-7 how the eighth notes and sixteenth notes appear first in one clef and then in the other, making both clefs alternately responsible for carrying the harmony (eighth notes) and melody (sixteenth notes) of the music.

Figure 15-7:
Excerpt
from Bach's
Fugue in C
Major.

Combining Forms into a Symphony

Literally, a *symphony* is a harmonious melding of elements. In music, a symphony is a piece of music that combines several different musical forms and is usually performed by an orchestra.

Traditionally, a symphony consists of four *movements* (self-contained sections inside a single musical piece):

- ✔ Sonata allegro, or fast sonata
- ✔ Slow movement (free choice)
- ✔ Minuet (a short, stately piece of dance music set in 3/4 time)
- ✔ Combination of sonata and rondo

The idea of a symphony is that it combines a multitude of musical forms harmoniously, so the aforementioned pattern is absolutely not set in stone.

The symphony form leaves the field for musical experimentation wide open. Some pieces that have come from this form are the most enduring and recognizable classical music pieces ever recorded. The most famous one, of course, is Beethoven's Symphony No. 5 (Opus 67), whose opening line, "Bu-bu-bu-BUM," is possibly the most universally known opening theme of any type of music. Figure 15-8 shows you the music for this legendary theme.

Figure 15-8:
Bu-bu-bu-
BUM. . . .

© *John Wiley & Sons, Inc.*

Observing Other Classical Forms

The classical forms in the following sections are enduring and important. They're more determined by how many performers are involved in the performance than the official structure of the music performed or the role of the performers themselves.

Concerto

A *concerto* is a composition written for a solo instrument backed by an orchestra. The concerto often creates superstars of classical music, such as pianist Lang Lang and violinist Itzhak Perlman. The soloists often carry as much weight as the long-dead composers themselves do.

Duet

Anybody who's ever sat through a piano lesson has probably played a *duet,* which is a piece of music written for two people. A duet generally consists of two pianists or a pianist and a vocalist. When other instrumentation is used, such as a bass and a violin, or some other combination, the term *duo* is most commonly applied.

Piano duets are most often used as teaching devices, with the student handling the basic melody line and the more advanced pianist handling the trickier accompaniment.

Etude

An *etude* is a brief musical composition based on a particular technical aspect of music, such as building scales, designed to help instruct the performer through musical exercise.

Fantasia

Fantasias are freeform and try to convey the impression of being completely improvised and divinely inspired, and are most often written for a solo instrument or a small ensemble. The modern equivalent of the fantasia is free jazz.

Chapter 16

Tapping Into Popular Genres and Forms

In This Chapter

▶ Dealing with the blues

▶ Topping the charts with rock and pop

▶ Kicking back with jazz

Discussing form when talking about popular music is tricky because the term is often misused. Think of form as being the specific way a piece of music is constructed, with governing rules to that type of music's construction (such as the classical forms discussed in Chapter 15). *Genre,* on the other hand, refers to a song's style, such as the instrumentation used, overall tone of the music, and so on.

However, some popular modern genres of music have been around long enough that specific patterns can be seen in their overall construction. These genres are:

✔ Blues

✔ Folk/rock/pop

✔ Pop

✔ Jazz

We go into more detail about these genres and forms in the following sections.

Feeling the Blues

The blues is the first truly American folk music (aside from the unique music that the Native Americans had before the European invasion). The structure of the blues is the common ancestor of pretty much all other constructions of American popular music and has been influential around the world. Around the turn of the 20th century, field holler, church music, and African percussion had all melded into what is now known as the blues. By 1910, the word *blues* to describe this music was in widespread use.

Blues music uses *song,* or *ternary,* form in three parts that follows an AABA pattern of I, IV, and V chords in a given scale. (You can read about song form in Chapter 14.) The B section is the *bridge,* a contrasting section that prepares the listener or performer for the return of the original A section. (Plenty of people complain that rock music uses only three chords: the I, IV, and V chords. Well, that all started with the blues!)

The blues is almost always played in 4/4 time, with the rhythm beat out either in regular quarter notes or in eighth notes and with strong accents given on both the first and third beats of each measure.

The most common types of blues songs are the 12-bar blues, the 8-bar blues, the 16-bar blues, the 24-bar blues, and the 32-bar blues. The "bar" refers to how many measures are used in each style of blues (see Chapter 4 for more about measures). If you're in a bluesy mood, check out the following sections for more on these common blues song types.

12-bar blues

The name is pretty self-explanatory: In *12-bar blues,* you have 12 bars, or measures, of music to work with. In each verse of the 12-bar blues (you can have as many verses as you want, but usually a 12-bar blues composition has three or four), the third 4-bar segment works to resolve the previous 4 bars. The resolution, or conclusion, to the I chord at the end of the verse may signal the end of the song. Or, if the 12th bar is a V chord, the resolution to the I chord signals that you go back to the beginning of the song to repeat the progression for another verse. If the song continues on to a new verse, the V chord at the end of the song is called the *turnaround.*

The most commonly used pattern — read from left to right, starting at the top and working down — for the 12-bar blues looks like this:

I   I   I   I

IV   IV   I   I

V   IV   I   V/I (turnaround)

So if you were playing a 12-bar blues song in the key of C, you would play it like this:

C   C   C   C

F   F   C   C

G   F   C   G/C (turnaround)

If you can hit those chords in that order, you have the bare bones for Muddy Waters's classic "You Can't Lose What You Ain't Never Had." Change the tonic (I) chord to an A (AAAA DDAA EDAE/A), and you have Robert Johnson's "Crossroads Blues."

If you're playing the 12-bar blues in a *minor* key, here's the common pattern to use:

i   iv   i   i

iv   iv   i   i

ii   V   i   v/i (turnaround)

Count Basie's famous and much-loved variation on the 12-bar blues took elements of both the major and minor keys, as shown here:

I   IV   I   v

IV   IV   I   VI

ii   V   I   v/I (turnaround)

8-bar blues

8-bar blues is similar to 12-bar blues — it just has shorter verses in it and a slightly different common use of chord progressions. Here's the standard pattern used for 8-bar blues:

I   IV   I   VI

ii   V   I   V/I (turnaround)

16-bar blues

Another variation on the basic 12-bar blues is the 16-bar blues. Where the 8-bar blues is four bars shorter than the 12-bar blues, the 16-bar blues, as you can probably guess, is that much longer.

The 16-bar blues uses the same basic chord pattern structure as the 12-bar blues, with the 9th and 10th measures stated twice, like so:

I	I	I	I
IV	IV	I	I
V	IV	V	IV
V	IV	I	V/I

24-bar blues

The 24-bar blues progression is similar to a 12-bar traditional blues progression except that each chord progression is doubled in duration, like so:

I	I	I	I
I	I	I	I
IV	IV	IV	IV
I	I	I	I
V	V	IV	IV
I	I	I	V/I (turnaround)

32-bar blues ballads and country

The 32-bar blues pattern is where you see the true roots of rock and jazz music. This extended version of the 12-bar blues pattern has the AABA structure, also called *song form,* that was adopted by rock bands in the 1960s. The pattern is also referred to as the SRDC Model: Statement (A1), Restatement (A2), Departure (B), and Conclusion (A3).

A typical 32-bar blues layout can look something like this:

(A1)	I	I	VI	VI
	ii	V	IV	V
(A2)	I	I	VI	VI
	ii	V	IV	I
(B)	I	I	I	I
	IV	IV	IV	IV
(A3)	I	I	VI	VI
	ii	V	IV	V/I

When it was first created, 32-bar blues wasn't nearly as popular with "true" blues performers as the 12-bar structure was, partly because it didn't work as well with the short call-and-response form of lyricism that earmarked the blues. It did work well for the country music genre, though, and Hank Williams (Sr.) used this construction in songs like "Your Cheating Heart" and "I'm So Lonesome (I Could Cry)." Freddy Fender used this structure in his hits "Wasted Days and Wasted Nights" and "Before the Next Teardrop Falls."

However, when this particular blues structure was picked up by people like Irving Berlin and George Gershwin; a lot — perhaps all — of the true heart of blues disappeared from the resulting music. The 32-bar blues transitioned into popular songs like "Frosty the Snowman" and "I Got Rhythm."

The 32-bar blues also was significantly altered by the intervention of other classically trained composers, who mixed the ideas of the sonata and the rondo (see Chapter 15) with the traditional American blues. The result was the eventual creation of non-bluesy-sounding songs that used such aspects of classical music as the ability to change keys during the bridge section of a song.

Having Fun with Rock and Pop

Most early rock and pop songs follow the structure of either the 12-bar blues or the 32-bar blues (see those sections earlier in this chapter). Chuck Berry's "Johnny B. Goode" is one variation of the 12-bar blues structure used in rock, as is the Rolling Stones's "19th Nervous Breakdown." The Beach Boys were masters of the 32-bar structure, using it in such songs as "Good Vibrations" and "Surfer Girl." The Beatles also used this structure in many of their songs, including "From Me to You" and "Hey Jude." Jerry Lee Lewis's "Great Balls of Fire," The Righteous Brothers's "You've Lost That Loving Feeling," and Led Zeppelin's "Whole Lotta Love" all also use the AABA 32-bar.

In 32-bar pop music, the music is broken into four 8-bar sections. Songs like Fats Waller's "Ain't Misbehavin'" and Duke Ellington's "It Don't Mean a Thing" follow the AABA 32-bar structure, whereas Charlie Parker took the rondo approach (ABAC) to the 32-bar variation in songs like "Ornithology" and "Donna Lee."

Compound AABA form really should be called AABAB2 form (but it isn't), because in this form, after you play the first 32 bars, you move into a second bridge section (B2) that sends you right back to the beginning of the song to repeat the original 32 bars of the song. The Beatles's "I Want to Hold Your Hand," The Police's "Every Breath You Take," Boston's "More Than a Feeling," and Tom Petty and the Heartbreakers's "Refugee" all follow this pattern.

The *verse-chorus* structure (also called ABAB form) is the most widely used form in rock and pop music today. Verse-chorus form follows the structure of the lyrics attached to it. You can, of course, write an instrumental piece that follows the same pattern as a verse-chorus rock or pop song, but the structure itself gets its name from the way the words in a song fit together.

Fender opens up the world of rock

The real break between blues and rock came when the first electric guitars hit the market in the late 1940s. Leo Fender built his first solid-body electric guitar, the precursor to the Telecaster, out of his garage in Orange County, California, around the same time that Les Paul was working on a similar design in New York. Both designs were loosely based on Adolph Rickenbacher's solid-body prototypes that had been making the rounds in the music industry since the 1930s. The electric guitar provided the opportunity to use such musical devices as *sustain* and *distortion,* which were previously unavailable to your average bluesman with an acoustic guitar.

Verse-chorus songs are laid out like this:

- ✔ **Introduction (I):** The introduction sets the mood and is usually instrumental, although sometimes it may include a spoken recitation, like in Prince's "Let's Go Crazy."

- ✔ **Verse (V):** The verse begins the story of the song.

- ✔ **Chorus (C):** The chorus is the most memorable lyrical points of the song — the song's *hook*.

- ✔ **Verse (V):** Another verse continues the story.

- ✔ **Chorus (C):** The second chorus reinforces the hook.

- ✔ **Bridge (B):** The bridge, which may be instrumental or lyrical, usually occurs only once in the song and forms a contrast with the repetition of verses and choruses.

- ✔ **Chorus (C):** The final chorus repeats the original chorus to fade, or it just stops at the I chord.

The typical rock and pop song structure, as we describe it here, is IVCVCBC. And just as in the 12-bar blues structure, the chords of choice are the I, IV, and V chords.

Thousands, perhaps even millions, of popular songs follow this structure. The Beatles's "Ob-La-Di, Ob-La-Da," Tom Jones's "Sex Bomb," Kenny Rogers's "The Gambler," Lady Gaga's "Poker Face," and Eminem's "Lose Yourself" are all examples of this structure used in contemporary pop music. The really amazing thing is how different from one another, either by virtue of lyrics or the music itself, one song can sound from the next.

Mark Mallman, musician, on the rules

Don't let theory bring you down. Theory is the tool that you use to get where you want to go. Just remember, you're the boss of your music. But at the same time, theory is a language that will enable you to communicate more decisively and more easily with other musicians. Sometimes, I'll find the need to bring in an extra bassist, and I'll get these guys whose technique is great, and they know all these tunes, but they have no theory training. I'll yell out, "Let's go up to the 5!" during the course of a song, and it takes them forever to figure out what we're doing, and I can't use someone like that. Every musician should know the basics of music theory, like scales, and how rhythm works, the really simple stuff that you can learn in a week. Knowing this stuff is like having all the secrets to making it through Super Mario Brothers. There's this magic that happens in a band setting when everyone knows where the other person is going with a song, and you can't have that magic without knowing theory.

Improvising with Jazz

The true spirit of jazz has always been improvisation, which makes identifying the actual construction of jazz most difficult. The goal in jazz is to create a new interpretation of an established piece (called a *standard*), or to build on an established piece of music by changing the melody, harmonies, or even the time signature. It's almost like the point of jazz is to break *away* from form.

The closest way to define how jazz is constructed is to take the basic idea behind blues vocalizations — the *call-and-response vocals* — and replace the voices with the various instruments that make up the jazz sound: brass, bass, percussive (including piano), and wind instruments, along with the more recent inclusion, the electric guitar. In Dixieland jazz, for example, musicians take turns playing the lead melody on their instruments while the others improvise *countermelodies,* or contrasting secondary melodies, that follow along in the background.

The one predictable element of music in the jazz genre — excluding *free jazz,* where no real discernible rules exist but jazz instrumentation is used — is the rhythm. All jazz music, with the exception of free jazz, uses clear, regular meter and strongly pulsed rhythms that can be heard throughout the music.

Part V
The Part of Tens

Enjoy an additional Part of Tens chapter online at www.dummies.com/ extras/musictheory.

In this part . . .

✔ Know the answers to frequently asked questions about music theory.

✔ Learn the different ways a musical score can be presented.

✔ Get the back story of some of history's most important contributors to music theory.

Chapter 17

Ten Frequently Asked Questions about Music Theory

In This Chapter

▷ Knowing what music theory can do for you

▷ Reviewing some of the top queries about music theory

*Y*ou may have skipped to this chapter just to see whether your top-ten questions match the ones listed here. Without the benefit of a write-in campaign, we can't possibly know exactly what's ticking away in all those musically minded heads out there, but we gave it a shot. With this chapter, we aim to answer ten questions we're most frequently asked about music theory, including why it's important to musical studies and what it can help you accomplish.

Why Is Music Theory Important?

Music theory helps people better understand music. The more you know about music theory, the better your comprehension of music, and the better you will play and compose (if that's your cup of tea). It's like learning to read and write: These skills can help you communicate better. Are they absolutely necessary? No. Are they tremendously helpful? Yes.

Here's just one example: By knowing how to read music, you can know exactly what a composer wanted you to hear in the piece of music he or she wrote down, no matter how many years separate the two of you.

If I Can Already Play Some Music Without Knowing Music Theory, Why Bother Learning It?

Plenty of people in the world can't read or write, yet they can still communicate their thoughts and feelings verbally. And, similarly, many intuitive, self-taught musicians have never learned to read or write music. Many of them find the whole idea of music theory tedious and unnecessary.

However, the issue is educational. Leaps and bounds come from learning to read and write. In the same way, music theory can help musicians learn new techniques and new styles that they would never stumble upon on their own. It gives them confidence to try new things. In short, learning music theory makes you a smarter musician, whether you're playing, studying, or composing.

Why Is So Much Music Theory Centered on the Piano Keyboard?

A keyboard instrument, such as the piano, has several advantages over other instruments — so far as composing goes, anyway. Here they are:

- ✔ **Everything you need is right there.** The main advantage of a keyboard instrument is that the tuning of the keyboard is such that the ascending and descending notes are laid out right in front of you in a no-nonsense straight line. Plus, early on when the piano was first created, the notes matched the pitch notations already being used in sheet music. So in order to go up a half step, you simply had to go over one key from where you started. This simple clarity was, and still is, extremely helpful in the composition process.

- ✔ **From the first try at playing, anyone can make musical noise on a keyboard.** With a keyboard there's no practicing with a bow, no learning how to properly blow over or into a mouthpiece, and no fingertip calluses that need to be built up.

- ✔ **A keyboard has a huge range.** No limit exists to how many octaves you can pile on a keyboard. The three to four octaves of the piano's predecessor, the harpsichord, were adequate to cover the range of music being performed in the 16th century. As the harpsichord quickly inspired instruments like the virginal, the spinet, the clavichord, and eventually the piano, more octaves were added to the basic form, until it became the eight-octave, concert-ready monster used today.

Is There a Quick and Easy Way to Learn to Read Music?

Does anything help make learning to read music any easier? Of course. All first-year music students are given a couple of cheesy mnemonics to help them memorize the lines and spaces of the treble and bass clefs.

Here are just a few mnemonics to consider (and if coming up with your own phrases works better, go for it!):

Treble clef (from bottom to top of staff)

Notes on the lines: **E**very **G**ood **B**oy **D**eserves **F**udge (EGBDF).

Notes on the spaces: **FACE**. That's it — everyone uses this one.

Bass clef (from bottom to top of staff)

Notes on the lines: **G**o **B**uy **D**onuts **F**or **A**lan (GBDFA).

Notes on the spaces: **A**ll **C**ows **E**at **G**rass (ACEG).

How Do I Identify a Key Based on the Key Signature?

Determining the key of a piece of music is a real doozie, especially for musicians who aren't comfortable following a piece of sheet music note for note but who want to *sound* like they know what they're doing right out of the gate — as opposed to noodling around until they figure out what the other musicians are playing.

If you know whether a piece of music is written in a major or minor key, you're on your way to determining the key. With a little practice, you can usually figure out whether a piece is in major or minor after hearing just one or two measures of a song. Here are some quick rules:

- ✔ If the key signature has no sharps or flats, the piece is in C major (or A minor).
- ✔ If the key signature has one flat, the piece is in F major (or D minor).
- ✔ If the key signature has more than one flat, the piece is written in the key of the next-to-last flat in the key signature.

✔ If the key signature has sharps, take the note of the last sharp and go up one note (changing the letter name). If the last sharp is D sharp, the key is E. If it's F sharp, the key is G.

✔ The relative minor of a key is a minor third down from the major. So when you move three adjacent keys, black or white, to the left — or three frets up the guitar neck (toward the tuning pegs) — you land on the relative minor.

For more on the major and minor keys, flip on over to Chapters 7 and 8.

Can I Transpose a Piece of Music into Another Key?

To transpose a piece of music into another key, you can simply move every note in the piece up or down by the same interval. For example, to transpose a song that you already know in the key of G into the key of C, you need to move everything up a perfect fourth or down a perfect fifth.

Another way to transpose a song is to learn the scale degrees of the original piece of music, and then play those same scale degrees in the new key. *Music Composition For Dummies,* written by Scott Jarrett and Holly Day (Wiley), goes into transposing music in greater depth.

Will Learning Music Theory Hinder My Ability to Improvise?

Learning music theory will absolutely not thwart your improv skills! Learning proper grammar didn't keep you from using slang or swearing, did it? Seriously, though, understanding the basics of music theory, especially chord progressions and scale degrees, will make playing with other musicians and improvising that much easier.

Do I Need to Know Theory if I Just Play Drums?

A lot of drummers, especially early on, take their role of being drummer to mean that they determine and keep the beat and that everyone else is following their lead. A really good drummer, however, realizes that he's also a part of the band. He acknowledges that in order to play with everyone else, he needs to know how time signatures and note values work and how to use tempo and dynamics to best fit each individual song just as much as everyone else in the band. A drummer who plays loud and fast or soft and slow all night for every single song gets boring. The guy who can mix it up and can play loud and soft *and* fast and slow adds contrast and makes the music that much more interesting.

Where Do the 12 Musical Notes Come From?

Many theories have been bandied about regarding the origin of the 12 notes used in music today. Some people think their origin is in math. The number 12 is easily divisible by the numbers 2, 3, and 4, which makes for an easy division of the tones between an octave.

Other theorists say that Pythagoras, a Greek from the island of Samos, had a cultural reverence for the number 12 and, therefore, made his version of the Circle of Fifths with 12 points on it.

If composers had strictly used the solfège model (see Chapter 19 for more on solfège) and abandoned Pythagoras's Circle of Fifths (check out Chapter 8), today's model would have nine points on it instead. The best answer to the question of the notes' origin, however, is from Schoenberg, who said a scale had 12 notes simply because 1 plus 2 equals 3. Many non-Western cultures have more or fewer pitches in their musical systems of scales and octaves.

How Does Knowing Theory Help Me Memorize a Piece of Music?

If you know scales, chords, and intervals, you can apply all this information to whatever piece of music you're learning to play. When you understand the form and compositional techniques used in a piece, it simplifies what you need to memorize for performances, both solo and in a group. Knowing how a musical piece is constructed makes it easier to anticipate what needs to come next in a piece.

Another good way to learn a piece of music is to divide the piece into smaller parts, and then play each of those small parts until you can play them from memory. As we discuss in Chapters 15 and 16, many pieces of music are composed of sections of music used again and again with only slight variations.

Chapter 18

Ten Keys to Reading
a Musical Score

In This Chapter

▶ How to read sheet music

▶ An overview of different types of sheet music

*O*ne of the main reasons that music theory exists at all is so musicians can write their compositions down for other musicians to play. Even if those other musicians have never heard the original piece, if they can read music, they can play the piece exactly how the original composer intended. As long as people know how to read musical notation, that piece of music can be played and replayed by musicians in countries around the world theoretically forever.

You can find many different ways to represent a piece of music, depending on how many musicians or musical instruments are involved, if the piece has vocals, or even if a complicated piece has been scaled down into something a beginning musician can play first time out. We summarize a few of the musical notations you might see in the sections below.

The Basics

While many of the basic music theory concepts seem to be almost universal, the way sheet music itself is written out generally follows the writing patterns of the society responsible for the creation. Therefore, depending on the part of the world the cartographer is writing music for, scores can be found that are meant to be read from left to right, from right to left, or in vertical columns. This book, however, concentrates only on the European standard of musical notation, which is always read from left to right, just like a piece of writing.

Lead Sheets

A *lead sheet* consists of the melody of a piece of music — usually something popular and easily identifiable — and most often just contains one musical staff. It often has the lyrics written underneath the notes, with the chord names or chord charts for accompaniment written on the top of the music. Lead sheets are a great, quick way to learn how to play a song on guitar. You can dig up a ton of popular music lead sheet collections, called *fake books,* out there for people who just want to know how to play their favorite songs without messing around with memorizing scales or reading notes.

Full Scores

A *full score* is a musical score that contains music for every instrument used in the performance. Generally, each instrument gets its own staff in a full score, because all the instruments are usually performing a slightly different piece than each other. You're most likely to see or use a full score for any performance that uses a large ensemble of musical performers, such as an orchestra or a marching band.

Miniature Scores

A *miniature score* is simply any musical score that has been reduced by a significant percent from its original size. But do not be deceived — this doesn't necessarily mean that a miniature score is small. Some printed miniature scores are as large as a regular music score, but have been reduced from a very large original score. Most miniature scores are made that way for portability reasons, especially the very large ones, and are very often made for purely aesthetic reasons for collectors of original musical compositions.

Study Scores

A *study score* is a printed score with additional academic markings and analytical comments added to the music. You're most likely to find study scores in anthology collections of sheet music.

Piano Scores

A *piano score* is, of course, a piece of music meant to be performed on piano. The music, which may or may not have originally been composed with multiple instruments in mind, is condensed or simplified to be contained in the treble and bass clef staves.

Short Scores

A *short score* is usually the first step for many composers to creating a full score. It carries the basic harmony and melody of a piece of music, upon which a composer can build on and expand into a piece for multiple instruments and voices. Most short scores aren't ever published or used by anyone other than the original composer.

Vocal Scores

A *vocal score* is music written out specifically for a vocalist, almost like a combination of a piano score and a lead sheet. The entire musical accompaniment is condensed to a piano score, with the vocal parts written out on separate musical staves and as words beneath the vocal section.

Tablature

Tablature, or tab, is designed specifically for guitar and bass. Instead of using notes, rests, and staves, though, tablature uses ASCII (American Standard Code for Information Interchange) numbers. These numbers represent the fret number to be played and are placed on four or six lines representing the instrument's strings. The limitation of tablature is that composers have no way to write specific note values, so often the pacing of the song is up to the musician playing the song, which can lead to many wonderful interpretations of the same piece. But the upside is that tablature uses ASCII characters, so writing out and sharing music with people on the Internet is insanely easy. You can get a ton more info about reading tablature in both *Music Composition for Dummies* by Scott Jarrett and Holly Day (Wiley) and *Guitar For Dummies,* 3rd Edition, by Mark Phillips and Jon Chappell (Wiley).

Figured Bass Notion

Figured bass is a little-used form of notation in which only the bass note of a piece is given, with numbers giving the interval quantity (scale steps) needed for the accompaniment written above or below the note. So, for example, if you have an F note written on a staff, with the numbers 6 and 4 written below that note, it would mean that the accompaniment should play a fourth and a sixth above the F (or a B and a D). Figured bass notation was used extensively in Baroque music and is very rarely used today.

Chapter 19

Ten Music Theorists You Should Know About

In This Chapter

▶ Seeing who had the most impact on music theory

▶ Considering music theory's evolution

*T*he evolution of music theory and notation is almost as amazing as the evolution of human writing. Modern music notation is sort of like Esperanto that lots of people can understand. People all over the Western world, and much of the Eastern world as well, know how to communicate with each other effectively through sheet music, chord theory, and the Circle of Fifths. In this chapter, we introduce ten music theorists who have helped define how we look at music or have changed our view of music entirely.

Pythagoras (582–507 BC)

Anyone who's ever taken a geometry class has heard of Pythagoras. He was obsessed with the idea that everything in the world could be broken down into a mathematical formula and that numbers themselves were the ultimate reality. As a result, Pythagoras came up with all sorts of equations for calculating things. He's particularly well known for his Pythagorean theorem.

The beautiful thing about ancient Greek culture is that the study of science, art, music, and philosophy were considered one great big pursuit. So it wasn't that strange for someone like Pythagoras to turn his attention to music and try to come up with mathematical theories to define it.

Because the lyre was the most popular instrument of the day, it's only natural that Pythagoras used it and other stringed instruments to create his working model for what would eventually be called the Pythagorean Circle, which then eventually evolved into the Circle of Fifths.

According to legend, Pythagoras took a piece of string from a lyre, plucked it, measured its tone and vibration rate, and then cut that string in half and made a new set of measurements. He named the difference between the rate of vibration of the first length of string and the second an *octave,* and then he went to work breaking the octave up into 12 evenly divided units. Every point around the circle was assigned a pitch value, and each pitch value was exactly $\frac{1}{12}$ octave higher or lower than the note next to it.

The problem with Pythagoras's Circle was that he wasn't a musician. Even though the Circle was mathematically sound and an amazing conceptual leap, some of the "tunings" he proposed weren't particularly pleasing to the ear. Also, due to variations in the size of sound waves that he (and everyone else who lived 2,500 years ago) wasn't privy to, his octaves quickly fell out of tune the farther you went from the starting point. For example, a high C, tuned to his perfect fifths, was definitely not in tune with a low C, because in his system you moved just a bit out of pitch with each new octave in between.

For the next 2,000 years, musicians and theorists alike concentrated on tempering this Circle, with its 12 spots and shape left intact, but they retuned some of his "perfect" fifths using *Pythagorean commas* to create a Circle that was much more musician- and audience-friendly. To check out the modern-day Circle of Fifths, see Chapter 8.

Boethius (480–524 AD)

If it hadn't been for the Roman statesman and philosopher Anicius Manlius Severinus Boethius, the Greek contribution to music theory may have been completely lost, along with much of Europe's own musical history. Boethius was a remarkable man who dedicated his short life to studying Greek mathematics, philosophy, history, and music theory. He was the first scholar after Pythagoras to try to connect the pitch of a note with the vibration of sound waves.

Not content to sit at home writing books, Boethius's most ambitious project was also one of his most enduring. He began venturing out into the western European countryside with music scribes who transcribed the folk music of the different groups of people that made up the landscape. Because of this work, you can still hear today what sort of music rural people were playing and singing during this time period.

Formal music traditionally didn't have lyrics; music with lyrics was considered lowbrow and aesthetically in bad taste. Ironically, his study of common music led to Boethius's exploration of writing songs with lyrics that told a story — an idea that would one day lead to a highbrow genre of music: the opera.

Sadly, before Boethius could write his own fully formed opera, or translate the entire works of Plato and Aristotle, or come up with a unifying theory to explain Greek philosophy (all three were lifetime goals of his), he was thrown in prison under charges of practicing magic, sacrilege, and treason.

Despite facing a death sentence, Boethius continued to write in prison. His last work was the *De consolatione philosophia (The Consolation of Philosophy)*, a novella-sized treatise about how the greatest joys in life came from treating other people decently and from learning as much as possible about the world while living. Well into the 12th century, Boethius's many texts were standard reading in religious and educational institutions all over Europe.

Gerbert d'Aurillac/Pope Sylvester II (950–1003)

Gerbert of Aurillac, later known as Pope Sylvester II, was born in Aquitaine. He entered the Benedictine monastery of St. Gerald in Aurillac when he was a child and received his early education there. Highly intelligent and a voracious reader, Gerbert rose up among the ranks of the monastery so quickly that rumors began that he had received his genius from the Devil.

From 972 to 989, Gerbert was the abbot at the royal Abbey of St. Remi in Reims, France, and at the Italian monastery at Bobbio (Italy). At St. Remi, he taught mathematics, geometry, astronomy, and music, incorporating Boethius's method of teaching all four at once in a system called the *quadrivium.* At the time, the laws of music were considered to be divine and objective, and learning the relationships among the musical movement of the celestial spheres, the functions of the body, and the sounds of the voice and musical instruments was important.

Gerbert resurrected an instrument from ancient Greece called a *monochord* for his students, from which it was possible to calculate musical vibrations. He was the first European after the fall of Rome to come up with a standard notation of notes in tones and semitones (half steps). He wrote extensively about the measurement of organ pipes and eventually designed and built the first hydraulically powered musical organ (as opposed to the hydraulically powered siren of the Roman arenas). It exceeded the performance of any other previously constructed church organ.

Guido D'Arezzo (990–1040)

Guido D'Arrezo was a Benedictine monk who spent the first part of his religious training at the monastery of Pomposa, Italy. While there, he recognized the difficulty singers had in remembering the pitches to be sung in Gregorian chants and decided to do something about it. He reworked the *neumatic notation* (early music markings) used in Gregorian chant and designed his own musical staff for teaching Gregorian chants much faster. He attracted positive attention from his supervisors because of his work. However, he also attracted animosity from the other monks in his own abbey and soon left the monastic life for the town of Arezzo, which had no official religious order but did have a lot of decent singers who desperately needed training.

While in Arezzo, he improved his musical staff. He added a time signature at the beginning to make it easier for performers to keep up with one another. He also devised *solfège,* a vocal scale system that used six tones, as opposed to the four tones used by the Greeks — *ut* (later changed to *do*), *re, mi, fa, so,* and *la* — to be placed in specific spots on the staff. Later, when the diatonic scale was combined with the "Guidonian Scale," as it's sometimes called, the *ti* sound finished the octave (later making *The Sound of Music* possible). The *Micrologus,* written at the cathedral at Arezzo, contains Guido's teaching method and his notes regarding musical notation.

Nicola Vicentino (1511–1576)

Nicola Vicentino was an Italian music theorist of the Renaissance period whose experiments with keyboard design and equal-temperament tuning rival those of many 20th century theorists. Around 1530, he moved from Venice to Ferrara, a hotbed of experimental music. He served briefly as a music tutor for the Duke of Este to support himself while writing treatises on the relevance of ancient Greek music theory in contemporary music and on why, in his opinion, the whole Pythagorean system should be thrown out the window. He was both adored and reviled by contemporaries for his disdain for the 12-tone system and was invited to speak at international music conferences on his beliefs.

Vicentino amazed the music world even more when, to further prove the inadequacies of the diatonic scale, he designed and built his own microtonal keyboard that matched a music scale of his own devising, called the *archicembalo*. On the archicembalo, each octave contained 31 tones, making it possible to play acoustically satisfactory intervals in every key — predating the well-tempered *meantone* keyboard in use today by nearly 200 years. Unfortunately, he only built a few of the instruments, and before his work could catch on, he died of the plague.

Christiaan Huygens (1629–1695)

Christiaan Huygens did as much for science and the scientific revolution of the 17th century as Pythagoras did for mathematics. Huygens was a mathematician, astronomer, physicist, and music theorist. His discoveries and scientific contributions are staggering and well known.

In his later years, he turned his immense brain to the problem of *meantone temperament* — a system of tuning musical instruments — in the musical scale and devised his own 31-tone scale, which he introduced in his books *Lettre Touchant le Cycle Harmonique* and *Novus cyclus harmonicus*.

In these books, he developed a simple method for calculating string lengths for any regular tuning system, worked out the use of logarithms in the calculation of string lengths and interval sizes, and demonstrated the close relationship between meantone tuning and 31-tone equal temperament.

As much as people in the scientific community applauded Huygens's genius, people in the musical world weren't yet ready (and still aren't) to give up their Pythagorean 12-tone scale. So aside from a few experimental instruments built on his calculations, the main principle adopted from his theories was to rebuild and retune instruments so that 12 tones could finally build a true octave.

Arnold Schoenberg (1874–1951)

Arnold Schoenberg was an Austrian-born composer who immigrated to the U.S. in 1934 to escape Nazi persecution. He's primarily known for his explorations of atonalism and 12-tone musical systems (or, serialism), but Schoenberg was also an accomplished expressionist painter and poet.

Schoenberg's compositions weren't well-received in his home country. The press there declared him "insane" after hearing a performance of "String Quartet #2, op. 10." His piece "Pierre Lunaire," which featured a woman alternately singing and rambling about witchcraft against a backdrop of seemingly competing instruments, was dubbed "creepy and maddening" by his critics in Berlin. His music, along with American jazz, was eventually labeled "degenerate art" by the Nazi Party.

Throughout his career, Schoenberg's work featured many firsts. His symphonic poem, "Pelleas and Melisande," featured the first known recorded trombone glissando. His opera, "Moses und Aron," was the first one to draw on both his experiments with the 12-tone series and on atonality. His most massive composition, "Gurrelieder," combined orchestra, vocals, and a narrator — over 400 performers were required for the original performance of the piece. Even today, his vibrant compositions feel disturbing, chaotic, beautiful, and amazingly contemporary.

Harry Partch (1901–1974)

At age 29, Harry Partch gathered up 14 years of music he had written, based on what he called the "tyranny of the piano" and the 12-tone scale, and burned it all in a big iron stove. For the next 45 years, Partch devoted his entire life to producing sounds found only in *microtonal scales* — the tones found between the notes used on the piano keys.

Partch devised complex theories of intonation and performances to accompany them, including a 43-tone scale, with which he created most of his compositions. Because there were no available instruments upon which to perform his 43-tone scale, Partch built approximately 30 instruments.

Some of his remarkable instruments include the Kitharas I & II, lyre-like instruments made of glass rods that produced gliding tones on four of the chords; two Chromelodeons, reed pump organs tuned to the complete 43-tone octave with total ranges of more than five acoustic octaves; the Surrogate Kithara, with two banks of eight strings and sliding glass rods under the strings as dampeners; and two Adapted Guitars that used a sliding plastic bar above the strings, with one string tuned to a six-string unison with a 1:1 frequency ratio and the other tuned to a ten-string chord whose higher three notes are a few microtonal vibrations apart.

Partch's orchestras also incorporated unusual percussive instruments, such as the sub-bass Marimba Eroica, which used tones that vibrate at such a low frequency that the listener can "feel" the notes more than hear them; the Mazda Marimba, made up of tuned light bulbs severed at the socket; the Zymo-Xyl, which created loud, piercing shrieks by vibrating suspended liquor bottles, auto hubcaps, and oar bars; and the Spoils of War, which consisted of artillery shell casings, Pyrex chemical solution jars, a high wood block, a low marimba bar, spring steel flexitones (Whang Guns), and a gourd.

Karlheinz Stockhausen (1928–2007)

Stockhausen's greatest influence as a theorist can best be felt in the genres of music that came directly out of his teachings. During the 1950s, he helped develop the genres of *minimalism* and *serialism.* Much of the 1970s "krautrock" scene was created by his former students at the National Conservatory of Cologne, Germany. His teachings and compositions also greatly influenced the musical renaissance of 1970s West Berlin (notable characters included David Bowie and Brian Eno).

In the long run, Stockhausen can be seen as the father of *ambient music,* and the concept of *variable form,* in which the performance space and the instrumentalists themselves are considered a part of a composition and changing even one element of a performance changes the entire performance.

He's also responsible for *polyvalent form* in music, in which a piece of music can be read upside-down, from left-to-right, or from right-to-left. Or, if multiple pages are incorporated in a composition in this form, the pages can be played in any order the performer wishes. As former student and composer Irmin Schmidt said, "Stockhausen taught me that the music I played was *mine,* and that the compositions I wrote were for the *musicians* who were to play it."

Robert Moog (1934–2005)

Although no one knows for sure who built the first fretted guitar or who truly designed the first real keyboard, music historians do know who created the first pitch-proper, commercially available synthesizer: Robert Moog. He's widely recognized as the father of the synthesizer keyboard, and his instrument revolutionized the sound of pop and classical music from the day the instrument hit the streets in 1966.

He specially designed keyboards for everyone from Wendy Carlos to Sun Ra to the Beach Boys, and he even worked with groundbreaking composers like Max Brand. Unfortunately, Moog wasn't the greatest businessman — or perhaps he was just very generous with his ideas — and so the only synthesizer-related patent he ever filed was for something called a *low-pass filter.*

When he first began building synthesizers, his goal was to create a musical instrument that played sounds that were different from any instrument that came before. However, as people began to use synthesizers to re-create "real" instrument sounds, he became disillusioned with the instrument and decided that the only way to get people to work with "new" sounds was to break away from the antiquated keyboard interface altogether. So his North Carolina-based company, Big Briar, began working on Leon Theremin's theremin design to create a MIDI theremin, which was designed to eliminate the interval steps between each note but still keep the tonal color of each individual instrument's MIDI patch.

Outside of building instruments, Moog also wrote hundreds of articles speculating on the future of music and music technology for a variety of publications, including *Computer Music Journal, Electronic Musician,* and *Popular Mechanics.* His ideas were way ahead of their time, and many of his predictions, such as those from his 1976 article in *The Music Journalist* that predicted the advent of MIDI instruments and touch-sensitive keyboards, have already come true.

Part VI
Appendixes

Visit www.dummies.com/extras/musictheory for an interesting article.

In this part . . .

- ✔ Find the audio track list.
- ✔ Take a look at chord charts.
- ✔ Review the glossary

Appendix A

Audio Tracks

° °

*T*he following is a list of this book's audio accompaniment tracks, which you can find on www.dummies.com/musictheory. You can download the tracks to your computer and listen to them as you read the book.

Table A-1		Track Listing	
Track	*Figure*	*Chapter*	*Description*
1		7	A major scale, piano and guitar
2		7	A flat major scale, piano and guitar
3		7	B major scale, piano and guitar
4		7	B flat major scale, piano and guitar
5		7	C major scale, piano and guitar
6		7	C flat major scale, piano and guitar
7		7	C sharp major scale, piano and guitar
8		7	D major scale, piano and guitar
9		7	D flat major scale, piano and guitar
10		7	E major scale, piano and guitar
11		7	E flat major scale, piano and guitar
12		7	F major scale, piano and guitar
13		7	F sharp major scale, piano and guitar
14		7	G major scale, piano and guitar
15		7	G flat major scale, piano and guitar
16		7	A natural minor scale, piano and guitar
17		7	A harmonic minor scale, piano and guitar
18		7	A melodic minor scale, piano and guitar

(continued)

Table A-1 *(continued)*

Track	Figure	Chapter	Description
19		7	A flat natural minor scale, piano and guitar
20		7	A flat harmonic minor scale, piano and guitar
21		7	A flat melodic minor scale, piano and guitar
22		7	A sharp natural minor scale, piano and guitar
23		7	A sharp harmonic minor scale, piano and guitar
24		7	A sharp melodic minor scale, piano and guitar
25		7	B natural minor scale, piano and guitar
26		7	B harmonic minor scale, piano and guitar
27		7	B melodic minor scale, piano and guitar
28		7	B flat natural minor scale, piano and guitar
29		7	B flat harmonic minor scale, piano and guitar
30		7	B flat melodic minor scale, piano and guitar
31		7	C natural minor scale, piano and guitar
32		7	C harmonic minor scale, piano and guitar
33		7	C melodic minor scale, piano and guitar
34		7	C sharp natural minor scale, piano and guitar
35		7	C sharp harmonic minor scale, piano and guitar
36		7	C sharp melodic minor scale, piano and guitar
37		7	D natural minor scale, piano and guitar
38		7	D harmonic minor scale, piano and guitar

Track	Figure	Chapter	Description
39		7	D melodic minor scale, piano and guitar
40		7	D sharp natural minor scale, piano and guitar
41		7	D sharp harmonic minor scale, piano and guitar
42		7	D sharp melodic minor scale, piano and guitar
43		7	E natural minor scale, piano and guitar
44		7	E harmonic minor scale, piano and guitar
45		7	E melodic minor scale, piano and guitar
46		7	E flat natural minor scale, piano and guitar
47		7	E flat harmonic minor scale, piano and guitar
48		7	E flat melodic minor scale, piano and guitar
49		7	F natural minor scale, piano and guitar
50		7	F harmonic minor scale, piano and guitar
51		7	F melodic minor scale, piano and guitar
52		7	F sharp natural minor scale, piano and guitar
53		7	F sharp harmonic minor scale, piano and guitar
54		7	F sharp melodic minor scale, piano and guitar
55		7	G natural minor scale, piano and guitar
56		7	G harmonic minor scale, piano and guitar
57		7	G melodic minor scale, piano and guitar
58		7	G sharp natural minor scale, piano and guitar
59		7	G sharp harmonic minor scale, piano and guitar

(continued)

Table A-1 *(continued)*

Track	Figure	Chapter	Description
60		7	G sharp melodic minor scale, piano and guitar
61		9	Intervals with a quality of fifths
62		9	Simple intervals in the C major scale
63		10	The root of a C major chord
64		10	The root and the first third of a C major chord
65		10	The root and fifth of a C major chord
66		10	C major triad
67	Figure 10-33	10	AM, Am, Aaug, Adim, AM7, Am7, A7, Am7(f5), Adim7, AmiMA7 on piano
68	Figure 10-34	10	AfM, Afm, Afaug, Afdim, AfM7, Afm7, Af7, Afm7(f5), Afdim7, AfmiMA7 on piano
69	Figure 10-35	10	BM, Bm, Baug, Bdim, BM7, Bm7, B7, Bm7(f5), Bdim7, BmiMA7 on piano
70	Figure 10-36	10	BfM, Bfm, Bfaug, Bfdim, BfM7, Bfm7, Bf7, Bfm7(f5), Bfdim7, BfmiMA7 on piano
71	Figure 10-37	10	CM, Cm, Caug, Cdim, CM7, Cm7, C7, Cm7(f5), Cdim7, CmiMA7 on piano
72	Figure 10-38	10	CfM, Cfm, Cfaug, Cfdim, CfM7, Cfm7, Cf7, Cfm7(f5), Cfdim7, CfmiMA7 on piano
73	Figure 10-39	10	CsM, Csm, Csaug, Csdim, CsM7, Csm7, Cs7, Csm7(f5), Csdim7, CsmiMA7 on piano
74	Figure 10-40	10	DM, Dm, Daug, Ddim, DM7, Dm7, D7, Dm7(f5), Ddim7, DmiMA7 on piano
75	Figure 10-41	10	DfM, Dfm, Dfaug, Dfdim, DfM7, Dfm7, Df7, Dfm7(f5), Dfdim7, DfmiMA7 on piano
76	Figure 10-42	10	EM, Em, Eaug, Edim, EM7, Em7, E7, Em7(f5), Edim7, EmiMA7 on piano
77	Figure 10-43	10	EfM, Efm, Efaug, Efdim, EfM7, Efm7, Ef7, Efm7(f5), Efdim7, EfmiMA7 on piano

Track	Figure	Chapter	Description
78	Figure 10-44	10	FM, Fm, Faug, Fdim, FM7, Fm7, F7, Fm7(f5), Fdim7, FmiMA7 on piano
79	Figure 10-45	10	FsM, Fsm, Fsaug, Fsdim, FsM7, Fsm7, Fs7, Fsm7(f5), Fsdim7, FsmiMA7 on piano
80	Figure 10-46	10	GM, Gm, Gaug, Gdim, GM7, Gm7, G7, Gm7(f5), Gdim7, GmiMA7 on piano
81	Figure 10-47	10	GfM, Gfm, Gfaug, Gfdim, GfM7, Gfm7, Gf7, Gfm7(f5), Gfdim7, GfmiMA7 on piano
82		11	Key of G major chord progressions
83		11	Key of C major chord progressions
84		11	Key of F minor chord progressions
85		11	Key of A minor chord progressions
86		11	Authentic cadence
87		11	Perfect authentic cadence
88		11	Difference between a perfect authentic cadence and an imperfect authentic cadence
89		11	Plagal cadence
90		11	Two more plagal cadences
91		11	Deceptive cadence
92		11	Half-cadence
93		12	80 beats per minute (00:00)100 beats per minute (00:12)120 beats per minute (00:20)

Appendix B
Chord Chart

*T*his appendix functions as a quick reference to the chords on the piano
and guitar. It covers all the keys and shows each key's chords to the
7th degree. We list the piano chords followed by the guitar chords.

The tricky thing about diagramming guitar chords is that the same chord can
be built in many ways, in many different places on the neck. To make things
easier, we include only chords that don't go beyond the upper seven frets of
the guitar neck.

For piano, the keys to be played in the chord are shown in gray. For the
guitar, black dots show you where to put your fingers on the frets. An "X"
above a string means you don't play that string. An "O" above a string stands
for "open," meaning you play the string but don't fret it. Also, for each guitar
chord diagram, the pitches for each open (non-fretted) string are, from
left to right, (low) E, A, D, G, B, (high) E.

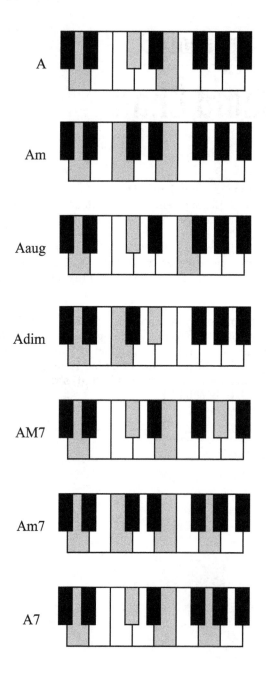

A

Am

Aaug

Adim

AM7

Am7

A7

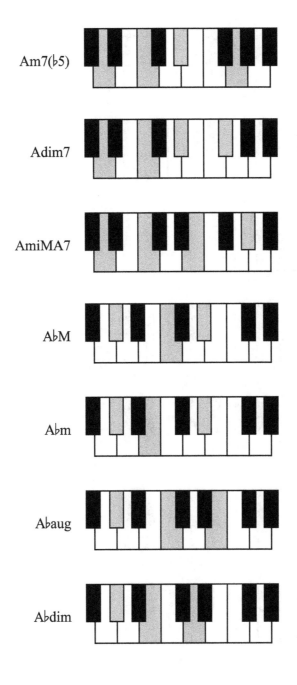

Am7(♭5)

Adim7

AmiMA7

A♭M

A♭m

A♭aug

A♭dim

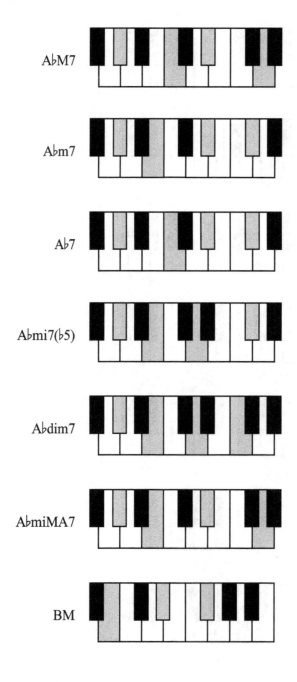

AbM7

Abm7

Ab7

Abmi7(b5)

Abdim7

AbmiMA7

BM

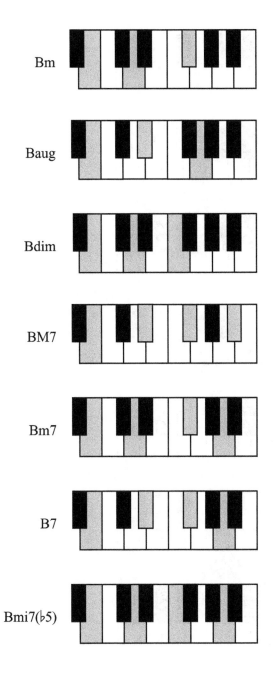

Bm

Baug

Bdim

BM7

Bm7

B7

Bmi7(♭5)

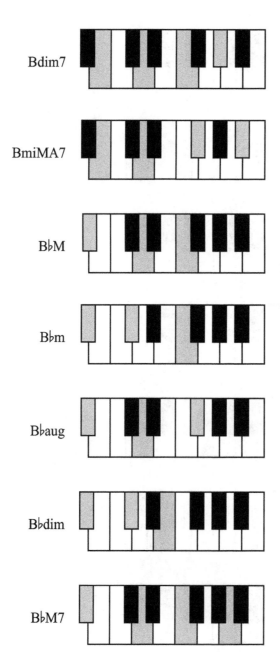

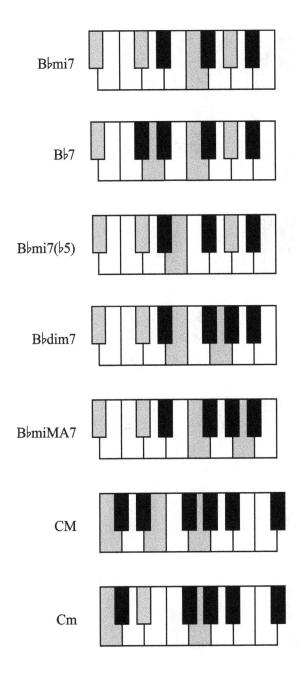

B♭mi7

B♭7

B♭mi7(♭5)

B♭dim7

B♭miMA7

CM

Cm

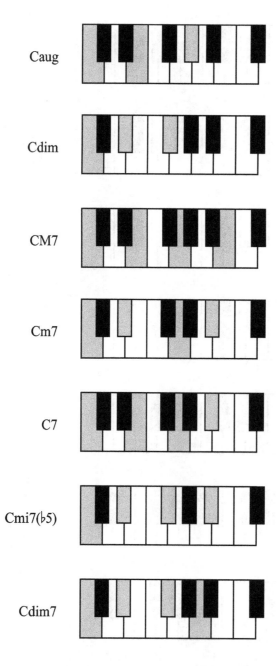

Caug

Cdim

CM7

Cm7

C7

Cmi7(♭5)

Cdim7

CmiMA7

CbM

Cbm

Cbaug

Cbdim

CbM7

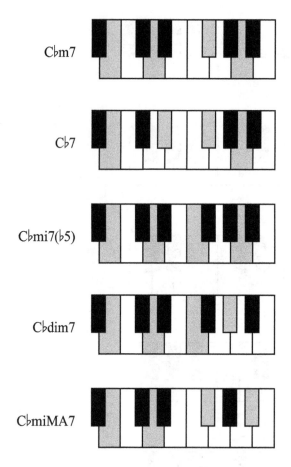

C♭m7

C♭7

C♭mi7(♭5)

C♭dim7

C♭miMA7

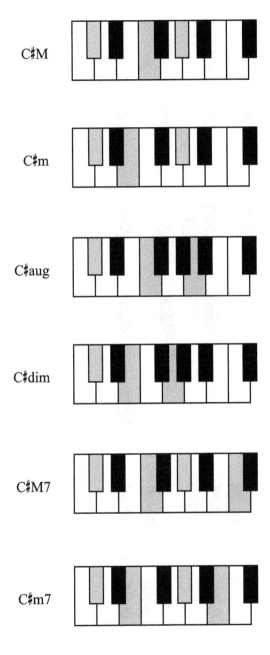

C♯M

C♯m

C♯aug

C♯dim

C♯M7

C♯m7

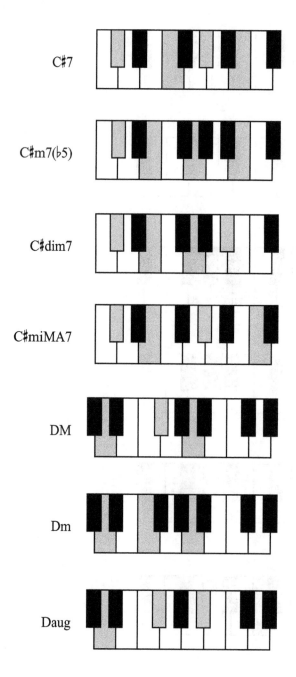

C#7

C#m7(♭5)

C#dim7

C#miMA7

DM

Dm

Daug

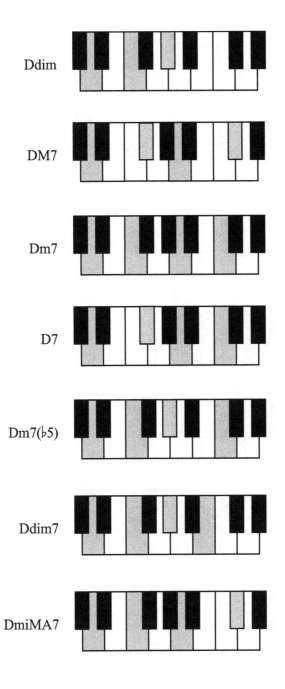

Ddim

DM7

Dm7

D7

Dm7(♭5)

Ddim7

DmiMA7

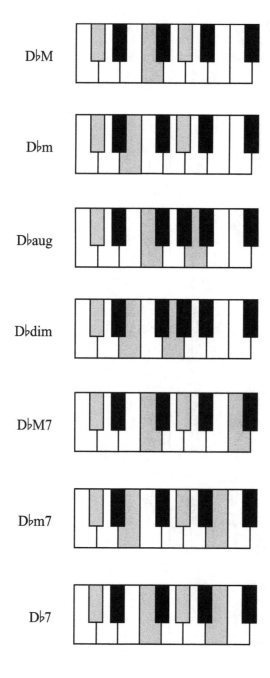

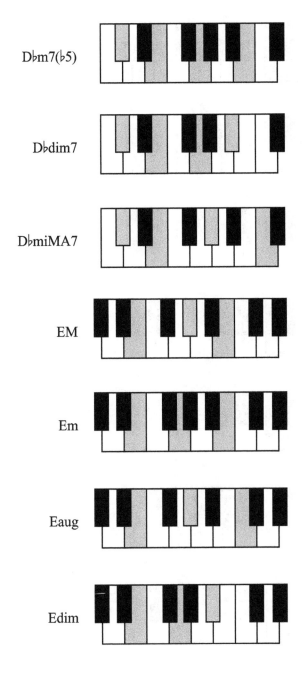

D♭m7(♭5)

D♭dim7

D♭miMA7

EM

Em

Eaug

Edim

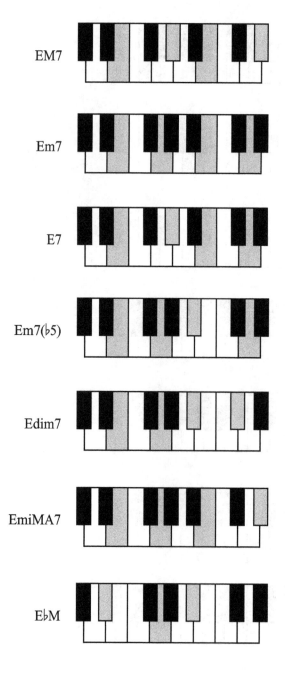

EM7

Em7

E7

Em7(♭5)

Edim7

EmiMA7

E♭M

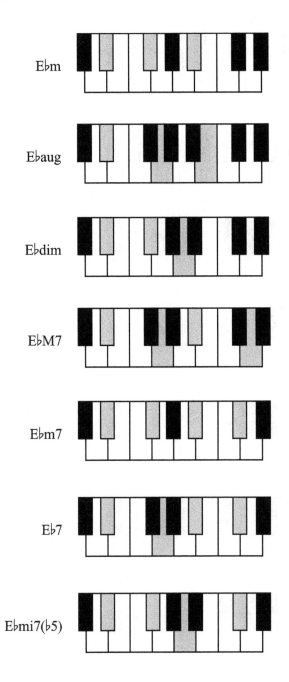

Ebm

Ebaug

Ebdim

EbM7

Ebm7

Eb7

Ebmi7(b5)

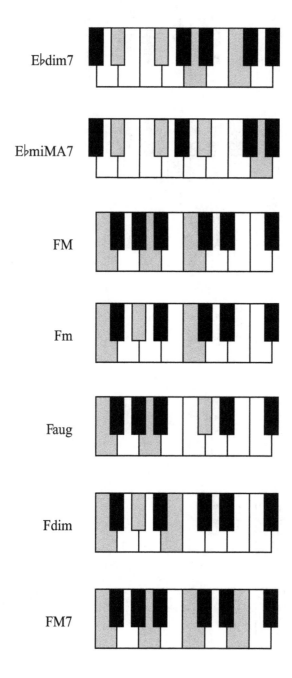

E♭dim7

E♭miMA7

FM

Fm

Faug

Fdim

FM7

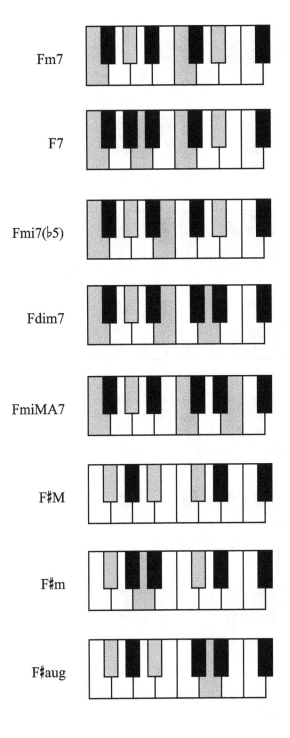

F#dim

F#M7

F#m7

F#7

F#mi7(♭5)

F#dim7

F#miMA7

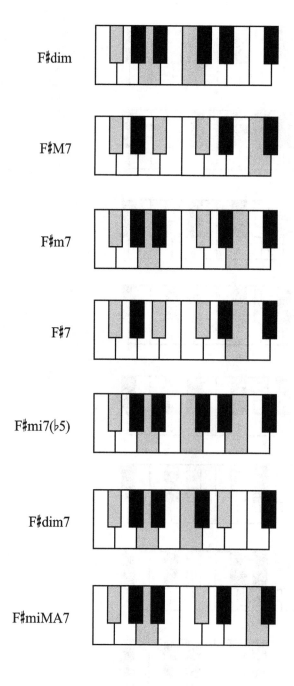

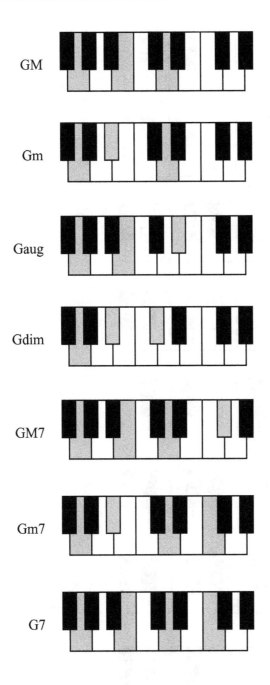

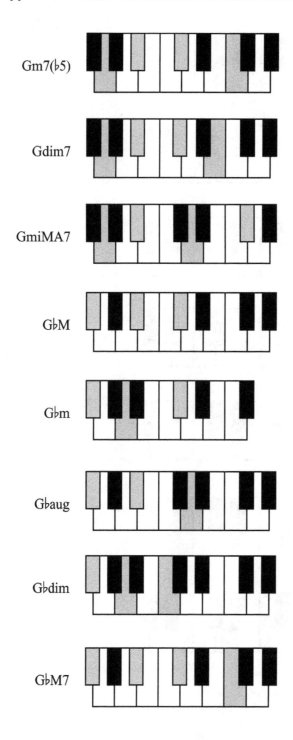

Gm7(♭5)

Gdim7

GmiMA7

G♭M

G♭m

G♭aug

G♭dim

G♭M7

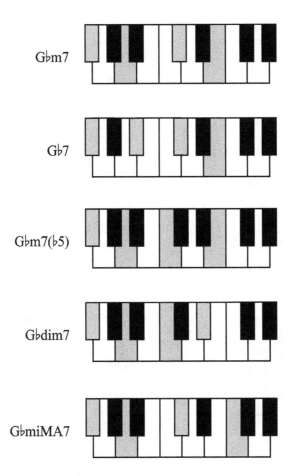

G♭m7

G♭7

G♭m7(♭5)

G♭dim7

G♭miMA7

AM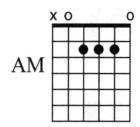

Am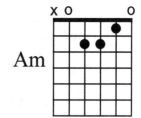

Aaug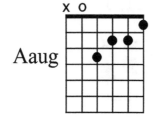

Adim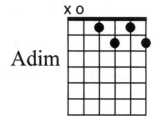

AM7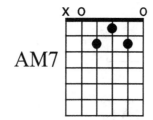

Am7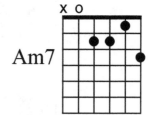

A7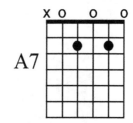

Am7(♭5)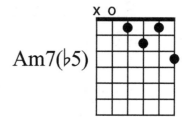

Adim7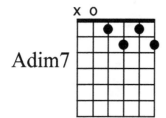

AmiMA7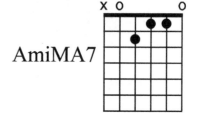

BM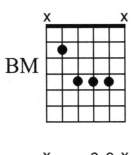

Bm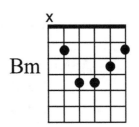

Baug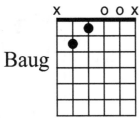

Bdim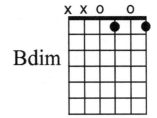

BM7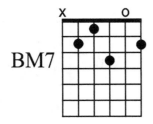

Bm7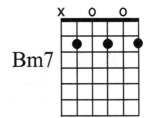

B7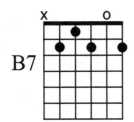

Bmi7(♭5)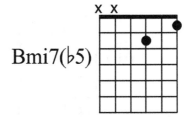

Bdim7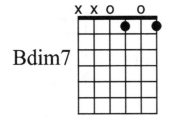

BmiMA7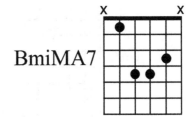

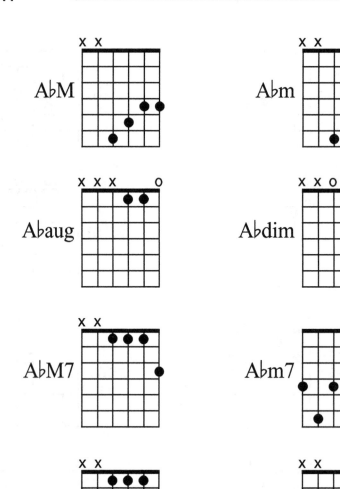

AbM

Abm

Abaug

Abdim

AbM7

Abm7

Ab7

Abmi7(b5)

← 7th fret

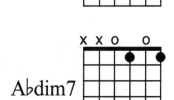

Abdim7

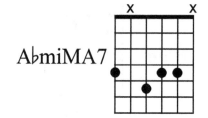

AbmiMA7

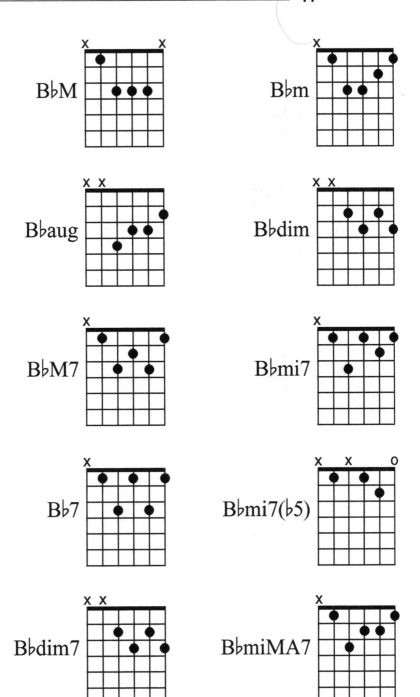

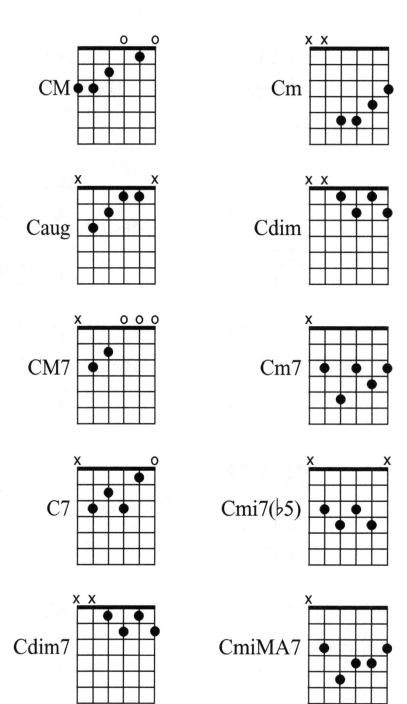

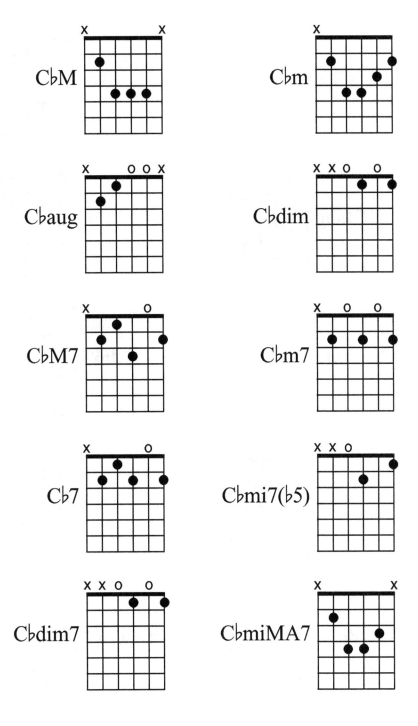

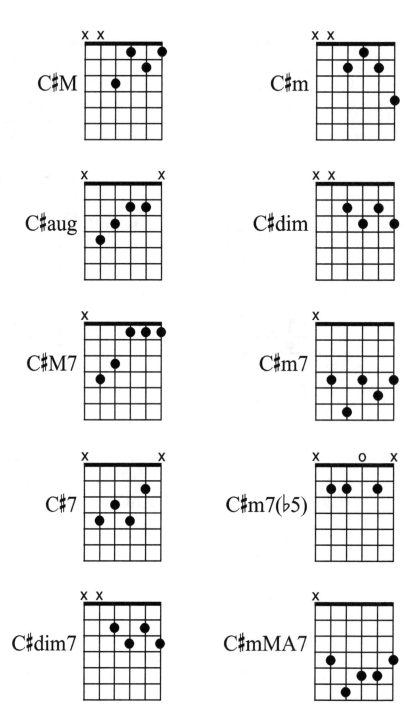

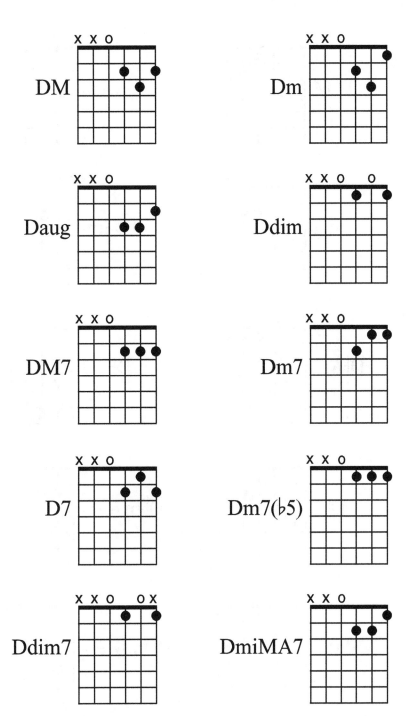

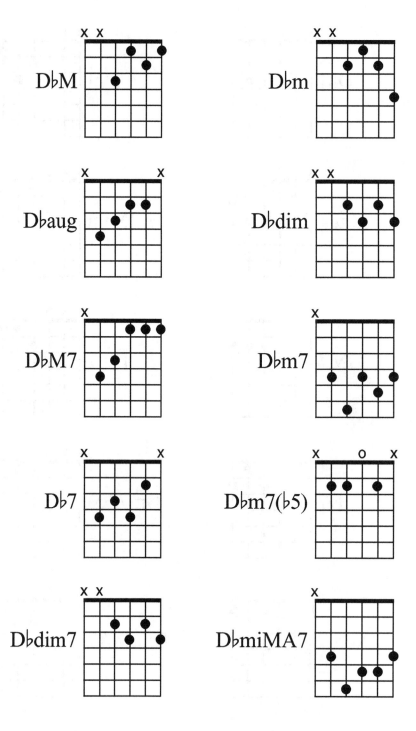

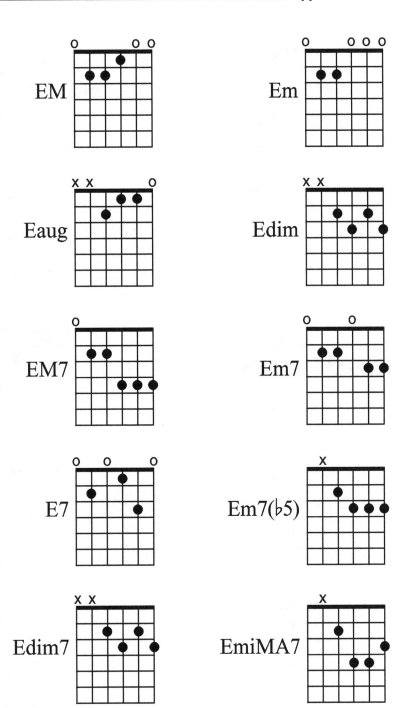

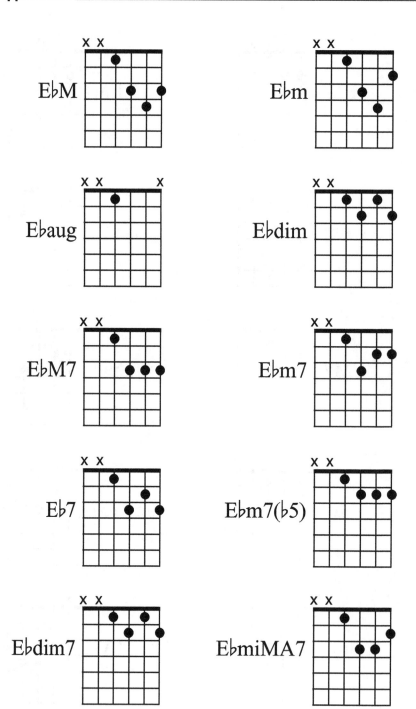

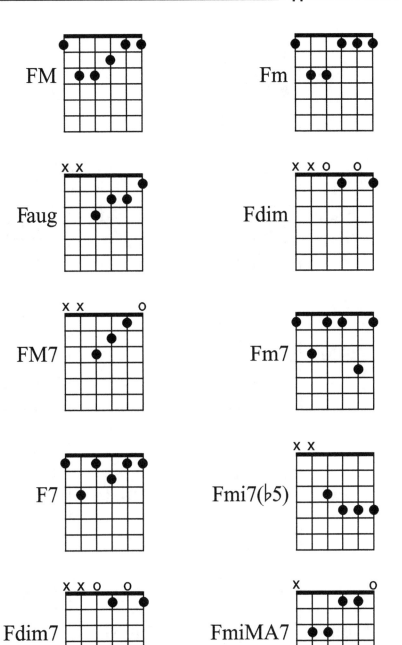

F#M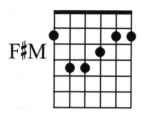

F#m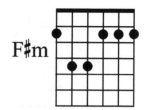

F#aug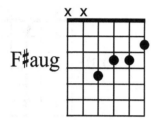

F#dim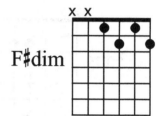

F#M7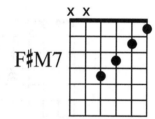

F#m7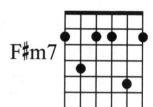

F#7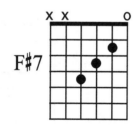

F#m7(♭5)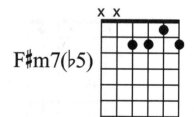

F#dim7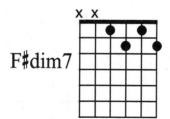

F#miMA7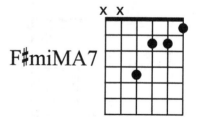

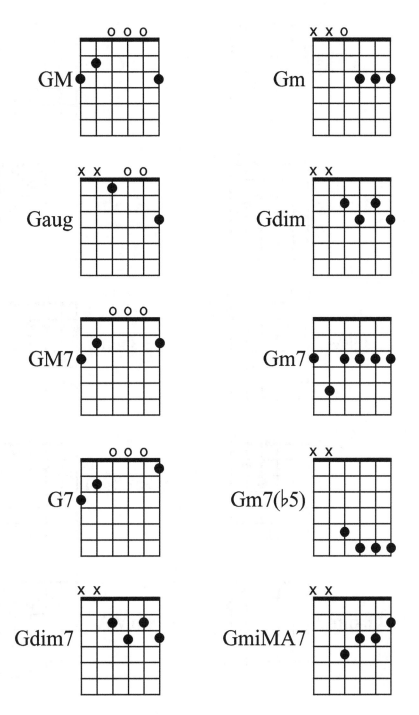

G♭M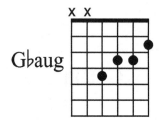

G♭m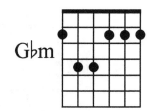

G♭aug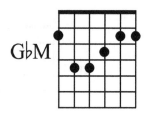

G♭dim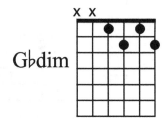

G♭M7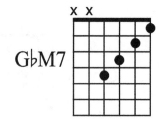

G♭m7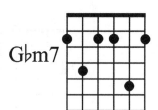

G♭7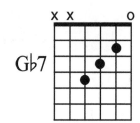

G♭m7(♭5)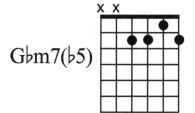

G♭dim7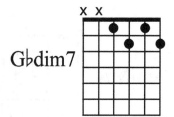

G♭miMA7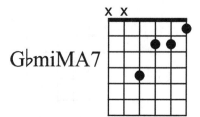

Appendix C

Glossary

accompaniment: The use of additional music to support a lead melodic line.

atonal: Music that is not in a key and not organized diatonically.

augmentation dot: A dot placed after a note or rest that extends its value by half of the original value. See *dotted note* and *dotted rest*.

bar lines: Vertical lines in written music that separate notes into different groups of notes and rests, depending on the time signature used.

bass clef: The lower staff in the grand staff. The bass clef establishes the pitch of the notes on the lines and spaces of the staff below middle C.

beam: A bar used (instead of a flag) to connect the stems of eighth notes and smaller notes.

beat: One of a series of repeating, consistent pulsations of time in music. Each pulsation is also called a beat.

bridge: The contrasting musical section between two similar sections of music. Also sometimes called the B section.

cadence: The ending of a musical phrase containing points of repose or release of tension.

call and response: When a soloist is answered by another musician or group of musicians.

chord: The simultaneous sounding of at least two pitches or notes.

chord progression: Moving from one chord to another, usually in established patterns.

chromatic: A musical scale with 12 pitches, each one semitone apart. See *diatonic*.

compound time: A meter whose beat count can be equally divided into thirds (6/8, 9/4, and so on) with the exception of any time signature that has a 3 as the top number of its time signature (as in 3/4 or 3/8 time).

cut time: Another name for 2/2 time.

diatonic: Conforming to the notes found in a given key. In a piece written in C major, for example, the C, D, E, F, G, A, and B are all diatonic pitches, and any other notes used in the piece are non-diatonic, or chromatic. See ***chromatic***.

dotted note: A note followed by an augmentation dot means the note is worth one and a half times its normal value.

dotted rest: A rest followed by an augmentation dot means the rest is worth one and a half times its normal value.

downbeat: The first beat of a measure of music.

duplet: A pair of joined notes used in compound time to divide a beat that should contain three equal parts into two equal parts.

flag: A curved line added to the stem of a note to indicate a reduced rhythmic value. Flags are equivalent to beams. See ***beam***.

form: The overall shape, organization, or structure of a musical composition.

genre: A style or manner of music.

grand staff: The combination of the bass clef staff and the treble clef staff. See ***bass clef*** and ***treble clef***.

half step: The smallest interval in Western music, represented on the piano by moving one adjacent key, black or white, to the left or right from a starting point, or on the guitar by moving one fret up or down from a starting point.

harmony: Pitches heard simultaneously in ways that produce chords and chord progressions.

homophony: Layers of musical activity, such as melody and accompaniment.

improvisation: Spontaneous musical creation.

interval: The distance between the pitches of two notes.

key (signature): The scale degree of a piece of music, which is normally defined by the beginning and ending chord of a song and by the order of whole steps and half steps between tonic scale degrees. (The key of C, for example, would be represented by the first C of the scale and the C an octave above the first.)

lead sheet: A scaled-down, notated melody with chord symbols, usually for rock or jazz music, which a musical performance is based on.

measure: A segment of written music, contained within two vertical bars, that includes as many beats as the top number of the key signature indicates. A measure is also called a bar.

melody: A succession of musical tones, usually of varying pitch and rhythm, that together have an identifiable shape and meaning.

meter: The organization of rhythmic patterns in a composition in such a way that a regular, repeating pulse of beats continues throughout the composition.

middle C: The C note located one ledger line below the treble staff or one line above the bass staff. See *staff* and *grand staff*.

notation: The use of written or printed symbols to represent musical sounds.

note: A symbol used to represent the duration of a sound and, when placed on a music staff, the pitch of the sound.

octave: Two tones that span eight different diatonic pitches that have the same pitch quality and the same pitch names in Western music.

pick-up notes: Introductory notes placed before the first measure in a piece of music.

pitch: The highness or lowness of a tone produced by a single frequency.

polyphony: Layers of different melodic and rhythmic activity within a single piece of music.

rest: A symbol used to notate a period of silence.

rhythm: A pattern of regular or irregular pulses in music.

scale: A series of notes in ascending or descending order that presents the pitches of a key, beginning and ending on the tonic of that key.

score: A printed version of a piece of music.

simple time: A time signature in which the accented beats of each measure are divisible by two, as in 4/4 time.

staff: Five horizontal, parallel lines, containing four spaces between them, on which notes and rests are written.

syncopation: A deliberate disruption of the two- or three-beat stress pattern, most often by stressing an off-beat, or a note that isn't on the beat.

tempo: The rate or speed of the beat in a piece of music.

timbre: The unique quality of sound made by an instrument.

time signature: A notation made at the beginning of a piece of music, in the form of two numbers such as 3/4, that indicates the number of beats in each measure or bar and shows which note value constitutes one beat. The top (or first) number tells how many beats are in a measure, and the bottom (or second) number tells which kind of note receives the count of one beat.

tonal: A song or section of music that's organized by key or scale.

tonic: The first scale degree of a diatonic scale.

treble clef: A symbol written at the beginning of the upper musical staff in the grand staff. The treble clef establishes the pitch of the notes on the lines and spaces of the staff existing above middle C.

trill: When a player rapidly alternates between two notes a whole step or half step apart.

triplet: Used in simple time to divide a beat that should contain two equal parts into three equal parts.

turnaround: A chord progression leading back to the beginning of the song.

whole step: An interval consisting of two half steps, represented on the piano by moving two adjacent keys, black or white, to the left or right from a starting point, or on the guitar by moving two frets up or down the neck from a starting point.

Index

About the Authors

Michael Pilhofer teaches music theory and percussions at McNally Smith College of Music in St. Paul, Minnesota. He has worked as a professional musician for more that 20 years and has toured and recorded with Joe Lovano, Marian McPartland, Kenny Wheeler, Dave Holland, Bill Holman, Wycliffe Gordon, Peter Erskine, and Gene Bertoncini.

Holly Day is a writing instructor at the Open Book Writing Collective in Minneapolis. She has written about music for numerous publications, including *Guitar One, Music Alive!, Computer Music Journal, The Oxford American,* and *Mixdown* magazine. Her previous books include *Music Composition For Dummies, Shakira, The Insiders Guide to the Twin Cities,* and *Walking Twin Cities.*

Dedication

To Wolfgang and Astrid, with much love.

Author's Acknowledgments

Special acknowledgement goes to all the musicians and composers who took the time out of their very busy schedules to share their thoughts on writing music with us: Steve Reich, Philip Glass, Irmin Schmidt, Barry Adamson, Jonathan Segel, John Hughes III, Nick Currie, Andrew Bird, Rachel Grimes, Christian Frederickson, Pan Sonic, Mark Mallman, and the late Dr. Robert Moog. A huge thanks to each one of you.

A big thank you also goes to the staff at Wiley: project editors Georgette Beatty and Tim Gallan; copy editor Sarah Westfall; acquisitions editors Tracy Boggier and David Lutton; and technical reviewers Karen Ladd. We thank our agent, Matt Wagner, as well.

Special thanks goes to Tom Day for mastering and producing the audio for the book and to rock poster artist Emek for continuing to inspire through his works.

Publisher's Acknowledgments

Acquisitions Editor: Tracy Boggier

Associate Editor: David Lutton

Project Editors: Georgette Beatty, Tim Gallan

Copy Editor: Sarah Westfall

Technical Reviewer: Karen Ladd

Project Coordinator: Melissa Cossell

Cover Image: © iStock.com/lillisphotography

CPSIA information can be obtained
at www.ICGtesting.com
Printed in the USA
LVHW060441271119
638510LV00007BA/119/P